e/.8

THE PHANTOM OF THE OPEN HEARTH

Also by Jean Shepherd

The Phantom *of the* Open Hearth

A Film for Television by
JEAN SHEPHERD
Co-ordinated by Leigh Brown

Doubleday & Company, Inc., Garden City, New York   1978

All of the characters in this book are fictitious,
and any resemblance to actual persons, living or dead,
is purely coincidental.

THE PHANTOM OF THE OPEN HEARTH was produced for Station
KCET/28's "Visions" series, Barbara Schultz Artistic Director, by the Television Laboratory at WNET/13 and the WGBH/2 New Television Workshop.

This screenplay is fully protected under the Copyright Laws of the United States of America, the British Empire, including the Dominion of Canada, and all other countries of the International Copyright Union and the Universal Copyright Convention. Permission to reproduce, wholly or in part, by any method, must be obtained from the author.

Library of Congress Cataloging in Publication Data

Shepherd, Jean.
    The Phantom of the Open Hearth.

    I. Title.
PS3569.H3964P5   812'.5'2
ISBN: 0-385-12976-9
Library of Congress Catalog Card Number 77–76280

THE PHANTOM OF THE OPEN HEARTH

An Introduction to the Film Script, by Jean Shepherd

The Phantom of the Open Hearth is loosely based on certain selected episodes from two closely related, previously published books. The first is *In God We Trust, All Others Pay Cash,* a novel, and the second is entitled *Wanda Hickey's Night of Golden Memories and Other Disasters,* which is, in effect, a sequel to the first volume. *The Phantom of the Open Hearth* is not an adaptation in any sense of the word, since the novel itself covers a much greater time span and has its own integral story line that is not found in *Phantom.* The same characters as in the novel are used, with some alteration.

I've always found that it is not a good idea to try to translate literally to the screen material that works very well on the printed page. For one thing, somebody reading a novel or a short story is simply not an audience. He is alone, and has even virtually eliminated his own body. He is a pure mind that has transported itself out of the here and now and is wandering in an imaginary landscape, eavesdropping on imaginary conversations and drawing its own independent conclusions. Somebody deeply immersed, submerged, in fact, in a novel is not even aware of people in the same room, or what time of day it is; if it is winter or summer, or if a tornado is coming over the next hill. This is why some people become virtually addicted to reading. It becomes a form of narcotic, and the greatest lead shield against reality that man ever created.

In a sense the movies are somewhat similar, but just barely. When I say "movies," I mean a film seen in its own environment, in a movie house on a large screen, with the accompanying aroma of popcorn and sagging seats. The very size of the screen itself, the overwhelming sound track, is enough to make many totally unbelievable scenes *seem* real, even though one little part of your mind keeps hollering "Baloney!" Nevertheless, in a darkened auditorium it is easy for most people to forget their own lives, scuttle their innate sense of reality and even accept as a true manifestation of religion Charlton Heston, dressed in a phony bearskin rug, standing on top of a phony plastic mountain, clutching plastic stone tablets. Even his complexion, of garish nondenominational orange, seems real enough as you squat in the darkness chewing your Butterfinger bar, engulfed by the booming voices and thundering studio orchestra.

Have you ever noticed that the great epics never seem quite as monumental when they're shown on the home screen in prime time as they did back in the old Orpheum? There are very good reasons for this. Some of them are obvious. Your Zenith Chroma-color has a wee twenty-one-inch screen that, compared to the vast expanse of beaded material used at the Bijou, is about like a postage stamp glued to the posterior of a bull elephant. You are indeed peering at Armageddon through a very tiny window.

In addition to that obvious fact, watching TV does not erase your corporeal self the way reading or going to the movies does. For one thing, few people turn out all the lights at home to watch TV. Half the time somebody in the room is doing something entirely different. He's not watching at all; maybe reading a paper or yelling at some friend on the phone. How long has it been since you have seen anyone read the sports page at the Radio City Music Hall, accompanied by Dustin Hoffman being pursued by evil Nazis? No, the home screen has its own conventions and any writer who is seriously trying to make a statement via TV, at least in the dramatic film, had better understand them and use them to his own advantage.

In *The Phantom Of the Open Hearth,* I tried to combine the techniques of all three media; the novel, the film, and TV. For that reason, we chose to do this work on film rather than on magnetic tape and to shoot everything we could on actual location rather than in the more conventional TV studio setting. I have noticed, for one thing, and this is a very personal observation, that every home that TV characters inhabit looks almost exactly like every other TV home that other TV characters inhabit. Mary Tyler Moore's apartment is the mirror image of Bob Newhart's pad, while in its rough outlines at least, Redd Foxx's house looks like where Archie Bunker hangs his hat. They all seem to have a stairway running up the back wall to an unseen second floor (Type A house, or Archie Bunker model) or they have a door which for some reason is raised up so that the characters enter and step down into the living room. This is the Type B or Mary Tyler Moore model. In all my years of living I have never even so much as visited in a home that has either of these two curious attributes. A rich and famous TV producer said, "I always put that stairway in there. Y'gotta give characters a good entrance," when I mentioned this to him. In other words, he was saying that the set was designed for convenience and technical reasons and certainly not for realism.

When *Phantom* was shot, we decided to go a different route and went scouting throughout the suburbs of Boston for a representative home that would fit not only the script, literally, but the typically American lower-middle-class mood we wanted. We also were working toward a feeling of twentieth-century timelessness. In other words, surroundings that not only existed in the past but still exist today and will continue to exist probably well into the next century, neither old-fashioned nor aggressively contemporary, and certainly not Archie Bunker kitchy. We avoided at all costs the kind of in-joke knee-slapper that some set designers seem to go for; the grotesque thirties lamp, the ugly forties dress line and the inevitable fifties leather jacket. We studiously side-stepped all the obvious TV and film symbols which constantly seem to pass for atmosphere on the screen, the sort of thing that completely destroyed, at least for me, *The Great Gatsby,* the film starring Robert Redford which piled 1920s cliché upon cliché until the essential tragedy of Gatsby was buried amid Stutz Bearcats, white flannel slacks and striped blazers. For me, a visual cliché is even more offensive than the verbal variety.

I often use verbal clichés in my work simply because many people in life really *do* use them. In fact, that's why they are clichés, but I use them deliberately to underscore a certain type of character whose life is built on the aphorism, the memorized joke, and the pious solemn Home Motto style of wisdom. From time to time my narrator in the script will use a high-flown cliché, but he does so with underlying self-mockery and a kind of tongue-in-cheek comment on the life and times of his filmic friends. In fact, the cliché is a powerful weapon if used properly *as* a weapon. On the other hand, a cliché, in the mouth of the wrong character can be the purest lead, especially if the writer believes he has just turned another deathless pearl of wit. In short, *use* a cliché; don't necessarily believe it.

The Steel Mill sequences, the actual scenes in the Open Hearth and including the ghostly shot of the Phantom itself, were in fact shot in a working steel mill, the Inland Steel Company at Indiana Harbor, Indiana, on the shores of Lake Michigan. Incidentally, the face of the Phantom is not a studio effect but is the actual eerie face that appears high up over the Open Hearth floor when a heat is tapped and the great gush of white molten steel roars out, throwing ghostly shadows over the girders and huge overhead cranes of the Open Hearth floor. I write this only because many people not familiar with the world of the steelworker have asked me about it and are always surprised to find that the superstition about the Phantom of the Open Hearth is a real thing among steelworkers, at least those fortunate enough to be around on the rare occasions when that ghostly face appears.

As to the actual writing of the script itself, many of the scenes in the script are very different from their counterparts in the novel, yet I feel that the essential mood and intent of the scenes remained intact. This was done in a number of ways. To get specific, the incident of the Gravy Boat Riot in the novel took place almost entirely in the mind of the mother. In fact, she never mentioned the riot at home, even after the police had broken it up. Obviously, a situation that takes place in a character's mind and is largely described secondhand by the narrator is not visual, even though the incident itself is highly so. Hence, I included Randy and the father in the final fiasco at the Orpheum to give the whole episode a feeling of completeness, of coming full circle.

Obviously, all of the time sequences were drastically altered. The riot was made to occur on the night of the Prom, which it certainly didn't in the book. The dramatic reasons for this time shift are obvious and evident and don't need much explanation, except to point out that the underlying theme of the script, the essentially commonplace, humdrum lives that the characters, and in fact most of humanity, live, are nonetheless not without their moments of high drama and Wagnerian disaster, all to basically no avail. This theme was much more dramatically underscored by having both events occur simultaneously and in two widely separated locations.

I can't speak for other writers, but in my own work I prefer never to editorialize on my characters, nor do I have my characters deliver sermons on the meaning of life; how sensitive they are, how all men must learn to love one another, etc. etc. which seems to be mandatory in what most critics call "the serious film." Is the mother happy with her lot, or unhappy? What about the father? Well, that's an interesting question. The father is no Archie Bunker, by any means. One afternoon when we were shooting a key scene, which I didn't feel was going right (it was in fact the moment when the father gives Ralph the twenty-dollar bill for his night at the Prom), I had a private discussion with James Broderick, the actor who played the father, about a specific and very pertinent point. I'll give you the scene the way we played it.

ME

Jim, why do you think he gives the kid that twenty-dollar bill?

JIM

Well, why not? He loves the kid, underneath it all, and figures he'd like to see him have a good time.

ME

Jim, do you think you'd mind if I asked you a question about this guy? I mean, it wouldn't break your concentration or any thing, would it?

JIM

I suppose not. Go ahead.

ME

Well, what do you think happens to the father after the end of this script?

JIM

What do you mean?

ME

I mean, say, two years later.

JIM

Hmm. I don't see what you're driving at.

ME

Now don't get mad. I'm just asking a hypothetical question. What happens to the family, say, two years from now?

JIM

I suppose Ralph goes in the Army or something, and the Old Man gets older, and maybe more unhappy.

ME

You mean, not much happens. They just go on.

JIM

. . . yeah. I suppose so.

ME

Would it throw your character too far off the track if I told you about what happens to him?

JIM

What's all this got to do with the Twenty Dollar scene?

ME

Plenty. You want to know what happens to the Old Man a year later?

JIM

Go ahead. You're the writer.

ME

(*studiously avoiding an obvious opening for a cheap shot*)

Okay. One year, almost to the day after Ralph's Prom, in fact the week of Ralph's high school graduation, the Old Man comes home, announces he's leaving the family, and takes off for Palm Beach with a twenty-year-old stenographer with long blond hair and a Ford convertible. They never hear from him again.

JIM
Good grief!
(*He was obviously agitated.*)

ME
He just ain't your average TV Daddy.

JIM
What's that got to do with the Twenty Dollar scene?

ME
Well, you think about it.

Jim went back to work and did the scene beautifully, very much sharper and more to the point than the way he had been playing it. There was suddenly an underlying hint of irony and even a little condescending savagery which had not been in the earlier run-throughs. The father in the script is, of course, fictional, but when I write, as well as when I perform, I carefully create in my mind a complete life history of the character I am creating or playing. It is a fact that we all are what we are at all times, which sounds like one of those Gertrude Stein non sequiturs until you examine it carefully. What I mean is, the father who gave Ralph twenty dollars on the night of the Prom was the same father who casually walked out on the family without regret a year later.

I've always been conscious of what seems to me a curious shallowness in most movie or TV characters. Does Archie Bunker ever leave Edith? No, not in TV land. It is only the young swingers who are allowed to divorce. Rhoda yes; Archie no; yet the divorce courts are crowded every day with people in their fifties and sixties who, after thirty years of marriage, are splitting because of blond stenographers and usually as the culmination of endless affairs. In fact, when I told Jim later that the Old Man was having an affair even during the period covered by the script, he made no comment, but I could see that it changed significantly his interpretation of the role.

On the other hand, there are some things you should never tell an actor about his character. For example, David Elliot (Ralph) asked me one day about the future lives of his character and his friends. Since they were playing their roles beautifully, I answered, "They make another smash film and get rich and famous." He laughed and went back to combing his hair, which he did incessantly. Actually, in the novel *In God We Trust, All Others Pay Cash,* Schwartz is killed in action flying a fighter plane. That's just the sort of thing you don't tell an actor about his character or that of one of his fictional friends. If you did, it would be inevitable that a hint of that tragic melancholy that actors love to play, those sad sweet smiles, would creep in, and forget the comedy. I did not tell Barbara Bolton, who played the mother, about her film husband's future peccadilloes, for the same reason.

Since this was a comedy, director Fred Barzyk and I worked together very closely on every scene. My humor is not the one-line insult-joke style of, say, *Rhoda* or *M*A*S*H* but rather humor that arises out of inflection, a character's attitude, the predicament he's in, and the constant struggle to remain afloat in a sea of petty disasters. Before each scene I would read the scene over in privacy with the director, reading line for line how each line should sound and even working with Fred on the visual humor, such as the episode of the tangled light cords during the Lady's Leg Lamp scene. Visual humor of that sort is almost entirely dependent on timing and meticulous editing and intercutting.

Later, in the cutting room, the three of us—Fred Barzyk, myself, and Dick Bartlett, as well as our associate producers Leigh Brown and Olivia Tappan—worked on these visual moments for hours. A film editor with a sense of humor is not only a plus in creating a comedy, but an absolute necessity. Bartlett's inspired use of the slowly moving empty swing when Ralph mentally gives up his dreams of glory and invites Wanda to the Prom was an editor's triumph.

I've always felt that most films fail to have a really solid core because there is no real single mind or will at work. The writer writes his script and is usually told politely to leave the premises. The director then proceeds to write *his* script, usually on top of and around the first script. Then the producer, with a bellow of rage and through a barrage of memos, proceeds to write *his* script, after which the star, through his agent and two lawyers, rewrites his role to suit his public image. And way down at the end of the line, the poor film editor tries to make a magnificent soufflé out of what is basically boardinghouse hash. The true forgotten man is the one who wrote the novel that the whole teetery structure was originally based upon. He more often than not winds up suing the lot to have his name removed from the credits, if they've even deigned to give him one in the first place.

In truth, many of the truly great films have been written, produced, acted, scored, and often even edited by one man. Orson Welles's *Citizen Kane,* Charlie Chaplin's *Modern Times,* Woody Allen's *Bananas.* The list goes on. In fact, Allen put it well when he said recently something to the effect that he writes, directs and acts in his own films because Comedy is so personal that he *has* to do it all to get the laughs that he knows are there. He's right. It is the only way that I find I can work. Fred Barzyk and I have worked together for fifteen years. He respects my control of Humor while I certainly respect his command of the technical side of production. Together, we work as one man. Leigh Brown, on the other hand, has worked with me for the same length of time and can sit back with a cool eye and see just when a scene or a line was played better, and why it missed. And there is no one better than Olivia Tappan at actually assembling the many various nuts-and-bolts of a production. Admittedly, this is a rare combination but I had to mention it here to answer whatever questions there may be about why we were able to convey so totally the essence and the spirit of *Wanda Hickey's Night of Golden Memories and Other Disasters* to the screen.

There were some cataclysmic moments. For example, during the actual filming of the Prom, Tobi Pilavin in the role of Daphne Bigelow showed up with a completely repellent hairdo that gave her all the charm of a spinster librarian going out for a big night at the Roseland Ballroom. This was completely off-kilter with the way I had visualized Daphne in the scene. The scene was written as a very impressionistic, surreal, almost dreamlike sonata punctuated with occasional blasts of cruel reality, i.e., Wanda's leering orchid, Ralph's sweaty back. For some reason everyone seemed to be about to film this sequence as a straight film of A Dance in progress; realistically, and with no flair whatsoever. The lights were too high, the band was playing something that sounded as though they were performing for a 1915 burlesque show, and it wasn't about to be much of a dream sequence.

I exploded. There were harsh, profane words exchanged. Actors cowered in corners. Rapidly my reputation as a Nice Guy went down the tube, and I was unmasked for the sonovabitch that I really am. All the while, money was ticking off the big Movieland taxi meter that drains the blood out of the American economy. Nevertheless, I was not going to allow the scene to be shot that way, since it was the key scene of the whole damn film, even if I had to hurl myself in front of the cameras every time they started whirring.

Ultimately the lights were lowered somewhat, the band stopped playing "Yankee Doodle Dandy" or whatever the hell they were blowing, Daphne's hairdresser allowed her hair to float romantically about her shoulders. Even then it wasn't exactly right, as far as I was concerned. I demanded a hand-held camera to be used so that close-ups, out-of-focus and otherwise, of Daphne floating alone around the dance floor, alone amid a sea of blurred faces could be shot. I sensed that they did it to humor me and to get the damn afternoon over with. Later, in the editing room, it was obvious that I had been right.

I use this illustration only to show that there are times when it is very difficult to get the precise effect that a writer envisions in a scene when he is creating it in his mind. After all, the writer can only put words on paper, and many scenes in *The Phantom of the Open Hearth* are not made of words but of mood.

The Prom scene is a great example of another technique I use in writing. I believe in always using what is actually available or what shows up accidentally during production, incorporating it into the script as much as possible. When I walked into the ballroom where the Prom was being held, I took one look at the gorgeously garish punch bowl that had been set up and I knew that it had to have a scene all its own. In addition, I also felt that the Dance sequence needed, dramatically, a break for the three principal male characters to meet and comment on what is going on. While shooting was progressing on the first half of the dance, I rushed into the next room and wrote a complete scene involving Flick, Schwartz, and Ralph at the punch bowl. In the white heat of excitement, it took maybe five minutes. The actors loved it and it turned out to be one of the best scenes in the whole Prom sequence.

In line with that technique, I always make it a point to write, in fact rewrite, scenes after the production has been *cast* and they begin work. Actors, after all, are not the characters that the writer originally visualized. I write dialogue for the characters I see in my mind, but when they appear in the flesh—James Broderick, David Elliot—and begin to speak, they don't speak the way the people in my mind did. Their voices are somehow different; their bodies move differently, so I carefully bend and twist the dialogue to suit them, always making sure that the scene's meaning and thrust and the essential character of the fictional people are never lost. This is probably the most difficult aspect of converting previously published material, i.e., a novel, into filmic terms. As a result of this technique, it was almost unanimously agreed by people who saw the film and who had read *Wanda Hickey* that the casting and acting were almost flawless. In actuality, I really cheated, I suppose, by carefully editing the published characters to fit the abilities and the assets of the actual actors.

In addition, certain performers gave me ideas for new aspects of their characters and I wrote additional scenes for them right on the set. During the shooting, Flick (William Lampley) emerged as such a strong character that his role changed drastically from the original unpublished script to the final version. In short, you have to work with what you've got and not what you wish you had.

Admittedly, the creation of *The Phantom of the Open Hearth* was an exception to the rule of conventional TV or film production. Barbara Schultz, executive producer of the "Visions" series, not only encouraged us at every turn but gave us a totally free hand, something most writers only dream about.

There's one technical note that should be explained, and that is the very difficult role of the Narrator in the script. The Narrator is actually the voice of Ralph, grown up, but at the same time he is somehow mysteriously in communication with the viewer. The viewer then becomes the second half of a dialogue between the Narrator and himself. The Narrator is both viewing the scene as it occurred or as he lived it and commenting to you about it, but never directly. He tells you, for example, what he thought at the time but not what he did, since you see that happening. He also makes oblique references to the ultimate consequence, in later years, of the action. This gives the script an added dimension of a life elapsed, and not just an isolated slice of time. The use of a narrator is a very special art and can be disastrous in a film. It can also, if properly used, add tremendously. It is particularly effective for a film to be shown on the home screen, which gets us right back to the old question of the difference between big-screen movies and TV.

When the film was finally finished, in the can, and we all went our separate ways, something happened to all of us that probably happens to all actors who involve themselves in something about which they care deeply. Films have a life of their own, and they send off sparks of that life into the participants. There will always be a little of Ralph now in David Elliot. Jim Broderick will forever carry around a bit of the Old Man in his soul. Tobi will be more Daphneish than ever, and Bill Lampley has been changed subtly since his meeting with Flick, while there is no doubt that Roberta Wallach, actually a lovely and sensitive girl, knows the dark side of the moon, which Wanda Hickey saw so clearly.

The entire film was shot in sixteen actual working days. Since we had a limited budget and every day had to count, the preshoot planning was as extensive and complete as we could make it. Every day's shooting was carefully planned out, practically minute by minute and for that reason things had to work the first time. We were lucky. For the most part, nothing went wrong, and only in rare, minor instances did we have to alter a day's planning because of unforeseen problems Nothing is as conducive to efficiency as a lack of ready money.

The film was finally aired December 23, 1976, over the entire PBS network of more than two hundred stations. It subsequently won a Television Critics Circle Award nomination for "Best Achievement in Comedy" and "Best Achievement in Comedy Writing," and James Broderick, who played the Old Man was nominated for "Best Comedy Performance" for the 1976 television year. It was the only film to be nominated that year in those three important catagories. Naturally, this included major shows from all the national networks. It has recently been selected by the Milan Film Festival as a nominee for Best Film and the Prix d'Italia. At this writing the film is scheduled for network-wide replays in the near future. It was extremely well received by audiences coast to coast and, all in all, we feel that we accomplished what we set out to do, which is about all anyone can hope for when involved in such a complex creation, which requires the talents of dozens of people and the skills of many artisans. I thank them all.

Jean Shepherd
Washington, N.J., 1977

THE PHANTOM OF THE OPEN HEARTH

CAST (in order of appearance)

Ralph as man	—	JEAN SHEPHERD
Ralph as boy	—	DAVID ELLIOT
Steel-mill worker	—	MICHAEL STEIN
Father	—	JAMES BRODERICK
Mother	—	BARBARA BOLTON
Randy	—	ADAM GOODMAN
Schwartz	—	BRYAN UTMAN
Flick	—	WILLIAM LAMPLEY
John	—	CARLTON POWER
Halfback	—	STEVE NUDING
Daphne Bigelow	—	TOBI PILAVIN
Wanda	—	ROBERTA WALLACH
Uncle Carl	—	ED HUBERMAN
Sherby	—	DAVID POKAT
Gertz	—	CHRIS CLARK
Ockie	—	JOE MAYO
Zudock	—	DAVID HOWARD
Teacher	—	MARY FENSTERMACHER
Deliveryman	—	JAMES BONNELL
Mr. Doppler	—	FRANK DOLAN
Al	—	JOEY FAYE
Morty	—	JOHN PETERS

Clara Mae	—	ANDREA MCCULLOUGH
Budge	—	PETER GRAHAM
Waiter	—	SOL SCHWADE
Lovely Arlita	—	LEIGH BROWN

Glossary of Abbreviations for Camera Directions

Abbreviation	Meaning
CU	Close-up
LS	Long shot
MS	Medium shot
POV	Point of view
SFX	Sound effects
MOS	Without sound
PAN	Camera sweeps from side to side, as in "Pan left" and "Pan right"
VO	Voice-over

A highway somewhere in America. We see a truckload of smashed cars traveling down the road. The cars fill the entire screen, seen from the POV of the driver behind them.

We hear the rumbling and roaring sound of the truck.

NARRATOR

(*over the roar*)
Would you look at that? How do you like that?

Super-CU shots of bumper stickers which fade in and out over traveling truck.

NARRATOR

(*VO*)
These old clunkers still got their bumper stickers on 'em. "Keep On Trackin'." What the hell does that mean?

Extreme CU of car bumpers.

NARRATOR

Hey, look at that. "Walt Loves Emily." Isn't that sweet? It's in Day-glo tape. Now there's sentiment for you. I wonder if Walt still loves her. Does Emily even remember Walt?

Camera pans past truck as driver/narrator passes.

CU driver. He wears sunglasses and cowboy hat.

DRIVER
Did I ever tell you about Daphne Bigelow? Ah, that's something I don't talk much about. I guess most men don't. You know, it all started for old Ralph here back in the Steel Mill country.

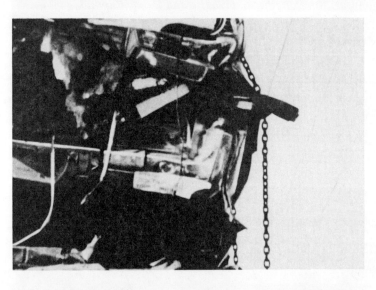

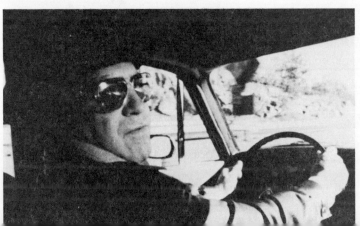

Sound of whistle blast going off.

Dissolve to steel mills in Indiana. They are belching out smoke that fills the air with a red dust.

NARRATOR
It all began here, in that great inverted bowl of darkness, that Stygian bowl of Omar Khayyam, the Midwest.

The camera moves past huge pipes and chimneys, trucking and panning, sweeping past a gigantic and foreboding living giant.

NARRATOR
Ah, my first real part-time job.

Camera discovers a young boy running. It is Ralph, the narrator, as a young man. Ralph is carrying a mail bag with the steel-mill logo stenciled on the side. He runs past steaming ingots, past signs warning of carelessness, past gigantic piles of scrap.

NARRATOR

(*over shot*)
Delivering the mail at the steel mill. The smell, the heat, the sounds . . .

SFX giant rumble and clash of machinery.

LS Ralph, running over crisscrossing railroad tracks.

NARRATOR

(*VO*)
Our town. *My* town, the very essence of the heartland of the industrial nation, where I learned to dream the American Dream of the beautiful future, the glorious past, and the crummy Now.

Ralph runs past fires and huge vats of molten steel. He shields his face from shower of sparks.

More sounds of steel mill and its surroundings; bells clanging, whistles blasting, dull roar made by furnaces.

Huge claxon sounds a warning. Workmen stop and look up. They gather in the darkened factory, waiting, as another claxon sounds. Ralph stops his running and stands next to a tall, strong, and laconic steelman. Organ music is heard, very dramatic, building up to a climax.

With the sounding of the last claxon, the heats are tapped. A large explosion, then a beautiful waterfall of molten steel cascades down into the open hearth.

CU of Ralph's face lit by the light from the molten steel.

CU of Phantom of the open hearth.

NARRATOR
The Phantom of the Open Hearth comes drifting out of the darkness when they tap the heat. Y'know, there's an old steelworkers' legend that says once you've stared into the enigmatic face of the Phantom of the Open Hearth, she will give you either good luck or bad luck—no one knows which.

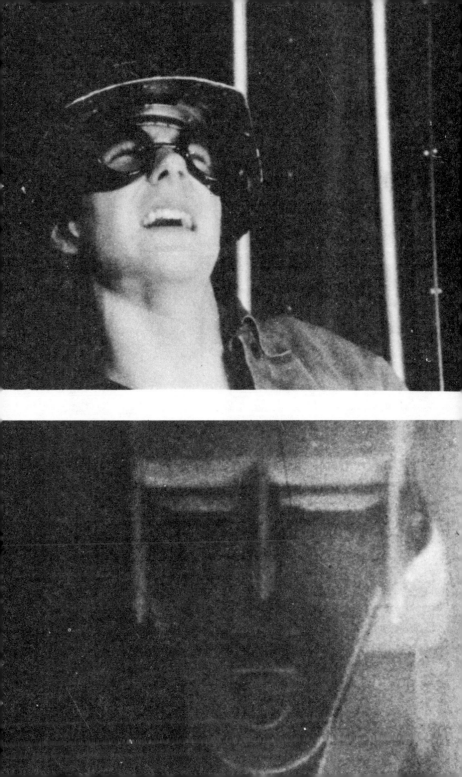

CU Phantom as camera slowly dissolves. Mat in credits.

Shot of the Old Man, Ralph's father, as he polishes his car. Music changes. It sounds almost like music that used to back up old-time newsreel clips.

NARRATOR
Ah, the Old Man, polishing his used Olds. You know, the Old Man loved used cars even more than he loved the Chicago White Sox, if that's possible.

The Old Man gets in car, starts engine. CU of rear of car. Car backfires with great puff of white smoke.

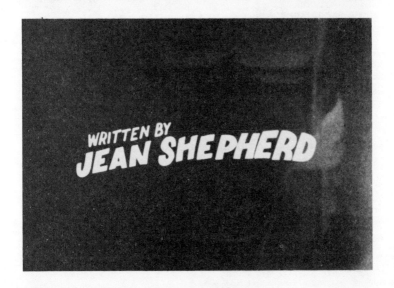

WRITTEN BY
JEAN SHEPHERD

Starring...

MS Mom, standing at the sink.

NARRATOR
My mother, forever battling the trivia of her life. The smell of red cabbage, meat loaf, and Jell-O in an endless stream.

CU small boy. He wipes his nose.

NARRATOR
My kid brother, Randy. His nose ran night and day. In fact, he could make it run at will.

Randy wipes nose. Camera switches to shot of rubber dagger.

NARRATOR

(VO)
He was also deep in his rubber-dagger period. He slept with it.

Organ music is heard, the Phantom's "theme song."

Upstairs hallway. Ralph comes out of bathroom, snaps towel at Randy, who is walking past.

RANDY

(running downstairs)
I'm gonna tell Mom!
We hear sounds of morning routine going on.

Ralph enters kitchen. The Old Man is seated at the table. Mom goes back and forth on an endless treadmill between the stove, the sink and the table. Randy slides into his place. The radio is blaring a weather report. Ralph sits down.

OLD MAN

Who're ya gonna take to the Prom, Axlegrease?

RALPH

Oh, I dunno. I was thinking of a couple of girls.

MOM

(*opening refrigerator*)
Why don't you take that nice Wanda Hickey?

Ralph turns, grimaces.

RALPH

Mom, look, this is the Prom. It's *important*. You don't take Wanda Hickey to the Prom. I got a coupla girls lined up, but, ah, well . . . Daphne Bigelow is at the top of the list.

THE OLD MAN

(*after a somewhat incredulous pause*)
Boy, you're really a glutton for punishment, aren't you? Well, you might as well learn your lesson once and for all. I mean, some guys grab the first skirt that shows up and they regret it for the rest of their lives.

CU Ralph.

NARRATOR
I suddenly realized he was talking about *himself*.

MS kitchen.

MOM

(*serving toast*)
Well, I think Wanda Hickey is a very nice girl. But of course what I think doesn't matter.

MS Ralph and Dad.

RALPH
I gotta rent one of those summer formals.

OLD MAN
Ya mean you're gonna wear one of those monkey suits?

RALPH
Yeah. Schwartz and I are going down to Hohman Avenue and check it out after school tomorrow.

RANDY
Oh boy, lah-de-dah.

RALPH
Hey!

He kicks Randy under table.

RANDY

(*whining*)
Owww!

LS outside of red brick school building. Teen-agers stand around, waiting for the bell to ring. We hear voices singing what is obviously a school song.

NARRATOR
The Prom, which was now two weeks off, began to occupy our minds most of the time. The semester had just about played itself out. Our junior year was almost over, and the Prom, oh, the *Prom,* was something that we had heard about since our earliest days. A kind of golden aura hung over the word itself. The Prom!

Interior school. Students hurry along the halls to their classes.

NARRATOR
There was only one thing wrong. As each day ticked inexorably by toward that magic night, I still could not steel myself to actually seek out Daphne Bigelow and ask her the fatal question.

CU beautiful girl standing under a tree. Her hair is long and golden, blowing in the spring breeze. This, obviously, is Daphne Bigelow.

NARRATOR
Daphne Bigelow! Even now I can't suppress a fugitive shiver of tremulous passion and dark yearning.

Beautiful harp music plays over extreme CU of Daphne.

NARRATOR

(continues)
There was something about her, something I'm not quite sure that I can adequately convey through the sadly lacking means of imperfect human language. Daphne walked in a kind of soft haze of approaching dawn. Daphne Bigelow!

Music changes from Daphne's theme to raucous restaurant-lunch-counter jukebox music.

CU hamburgers sizzling on greasy grill.

Pull back to see John's Place, which caters to the high school crowd. Two boys sit at counter, talking. Ralph enters.

NARRATOR
Ah, Flick and Schwartz, my two bosom buddies. Flick, skinny and mean, with the mind of a weasel. Schwartz, round and jovial, with the mind of a pumpkin.

Ralph joins his friends.

SCHWARTZ

(*mouth full of french fries*)
I bet you couldn't guess what I'm getting for my birthday.

RALPH

(*absently*)
Hmm?

FLICK
Hey, John, gimme a hotdog with french fries and a Coke.

More conversation among the three friends.

SCHWARTZ
You're never gonna guess what. . . .

RALPH

(*bored*)
Yeah, I know, I probably won't.

FLICK
Ah, this ketchup is rotten. It's all clotted on the bottom.

Flick waves ketchup bottle.

FLICK

Hey, John, a little fresh ketchup over here? This bottle's been on the table for about six years.

John turns, a short, swarthy man of uncertain parentage and evil temper due to a life of continual harassment by acne-plagued adolescents and a succession of short-order cooks who quit every three days.

JOHN

Who the hell's callin' for ketchup?

FLICK

Me, over here.

Camera pans over beautiful, scenic John's Lunchroom, picking up details. Humorous signs on walls, poster advertising pancakes, etc.

NARRATOR

John's. What a joint. John hated kids. He always dreamed of having a great truck stop, and what did he get? Millions of kids.

SCHWARTZ

It's gonna be some birthday, Ralph.

RALPH

Yeah.

SCHWARTZ

What's the matter with you, you got the crud or something?

Flick turns.

FLICK

Ya got the crud? Stay away from me, man. I don't need no crud.

RALPH

Who's got the crud? Listen, let's get a booth, huh?

They cross lunchroom, scramble into empty booth. John brings their order.

JOHN

(*surly*)
Who gets the coffee malt?

FLICK
Here.

JOHN
You two get the Cokes, right?

RALPH AND SCHWARTZ
Yeah, yeah. . . .

John serves their order. Ralph picks up Coke bottle, takes long swig.

SCHWARTZ
Hey Ralph, you going to the Prom?

RALPH

(*around Coke bottle*)
Uh huh.

Flick leans forward intently.

FLICK
Who ya takin'?

Ralph shrugs. Very casual, very debonair.

RALPH
Daphne Bigelow.

Schwartz and Flick register stunned amazement. The school's star halfback, who just happens to be passing their table, pauses, smiles.

HALFBACK
Did you say "Bigelow," kid?

RALPH
Yeah.

HALFBACK
(*sneering chuckles*)
That's what I thought you said.

Halfback leaves. Flick, Schwartz, and Ralph look after him.

SCHWARTZ
(*puzzled*)
What was that all about?

RALPH
Damned if I know.

FLICK
Ya never know with them jocks.

Dissolve to exterior white frame house. Used Oldsmobile is parked in driveway. Small boy, Randy, comes running around from back. He gallops up front steps, thrusts hand into mailbox, pulls out letter.

We see the Old Man walking up the front walk.

RANDY
Hey, Dad! A letter.

OLD MAN
No kidding?

RANDY
What is it?

OLD MAN
Nothing good, I'll bet.

Randy runs inside, shouting.

RANDY
Hey, Mom, Dad's got a letter.

OLD MAN

(*yelling*)
Don't leave the screen door open!

MS Mom, in kitchen as usual. She turns from sink, wipes hands on dish towel.

MOM
What did you say, Randy?

RANDY
Dad's got a letter.

MOM
Oh.

Old Man stands in kitchen, opens letter. His face remains impassive, almost as if he is too stunned by the gigantic import of receiving the letter to actually comprehend its content.

OLD MAN
Listen to this . . .

He reads, flat voice, reading by rote.
Congratulations, you have won a major award in our fifty-thousand-dollar Great Heroes from the World of Sports contest.

(*organ music*)

OLD MAN

(*continues*)
It will arrive by special messenger delivered to your address. (*He pauses*) You are a *winner*. Congratulations.

The Old Man and Mom exchange long, meaningful looks. He looks stunned; she appears merely confused. The organ music rises as the scene dissolves to:

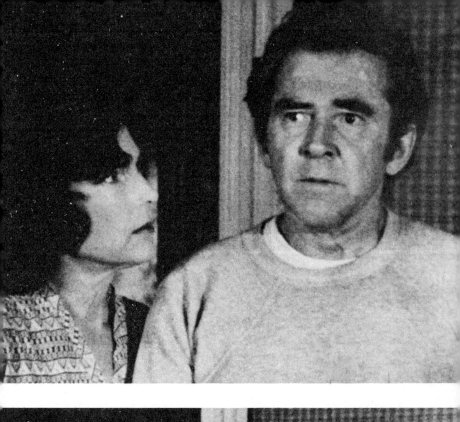

Exterior of grocery store. A short, unattractive girl with thick glasses and dark, furry hair is seen walking down the wooden steps, carrying a paper bag of groceries.

Ralph is passing, walking slowly, his hands jammed into his pockets. He appears bemused, lost in thought; fevered dreams of Daphne, no doubt.

WANDA

(*brightly*)
Hi, Ralph!

RALPH

(*absently*)
Hi, Wanda.

Wanda falls into step beside him. Ralph ignores her.

WANDA
Do you have to work today?

RALPH
I already did. You know, half a day on Saturday.

WANDA
Oh. (*She brightens again*) Want a jawbreaker?

RALPH
Yeah. Thanks.

They continue walking down street, both sucking on jawbreakers.

NARRATOR
(*sardonically*)
Of all the girls to like me! Wanda Hickey. What a bummer. Ever since we'd been in third grade, Wanda had just been hanging around. Once, when we were twelve, she sent me a Valentine. It had paper lace and bare-bottomed Cupids, oh ugh. She wore glasses that reminded you of the bottoms of Coke bottles. Wanda Hickey, the algebra shark.

WANDA
Well, I've got to go.

RALPH
(*disinterested*)
See ya.

Interior, front hallway. The Old Man is talking on the phone.

NARRATOR
The Old Man was a winner.

OLD MAN
Mr. Smothers?

NARRATOR
(*As narrator is speaking, we can hear the voice of the Old Man as he is talking on the phone*)
Real estate agents and used car salesmen started calling, making helpful suggestions for highly rewarding investments.

OLD MAN
(*savoring his moment in the sun*)
You would like me to invest in a *tombstone* company? No. (*A short pause*) No.

Sounds of laughter and merrymaking. The scene shifts to the living room. The Old Man and his friends are celebrating. The Old Man hands out Pabst Blue Ribbon to all the guys.

OCKIE
Boy, that musta really been tough.

OLD MAN
It was easy, really. The first week was Bill Tilden, Babe Ruth, Man O' War and the Fighting Irish.

GERTZ
Hey, it says here that you're eligible for a Grand Prize of fifty thousand bucks, plus . . . (*he trails off*) hundreds of additional . . .

SHERBY
I never won a thing. But I'm good at finding the Hidden Object.

OLD MAN
Lissen, lissen, seeing as how I am the winner of the jackpot, having been judged on . . . ah . . . originality, neatness, and aptness of thought—and of course all decisions are final— I would like to propose a toast. (*Yelling*) Hey, Ralph . . . get that bottle of NeHi.

NARRATOR
The party was really warming up.

OLD MAN
I wanna propose a toast!

Ralph runs to kitchen, takes bottle of pop from refrigerator, looks for opener.

NARRATOR

There it was. NeHi Orange. It was so spectacularly gassy that violent cases of the bends were common among those who gulped it down too fast. It would clean out your sinuses faster than a Roto-Rooter.

Mom is now on the phone in the hallway. In the background, through the living-room door, we can see the beery celebration going full blast.

MOM

No, it just came today. Yes, about noon.

Ralph runs back into living room, hands NeHi bottle to the Old Man.

OLD MAN

To NeHi, the best orange pop that ever ran a contest.

He holds bottle up triumphantly.
To the pop that made me a Winner.

Friends laugh and cheer him on as Old Man chugs bottle of pop. He drains bottle, gasps, smiles, belches.

Suddenly from outside comes the blowing of someone's car horn. The revelers rush to the window.

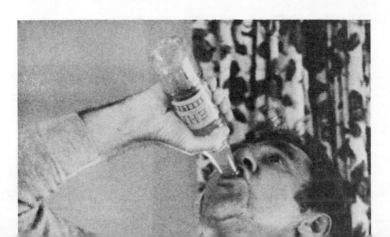

GERTZ
Ah, it's Zudock.

Cut to an ancient truck making its way up to the porch. Zudock, the driver, goes over part of the lawn, driving as if in an emergency.

Everybody rushes outside, yelling and laughing, greeting Zudock. Nobody is listening to anyone else, waving beer bottles, etc.

ZUDOCK

(*yelling to the guys on porch*)
Knock it off, knock it off. I got something important to say!

GERTZ
Ah shoot, Zudock, you ain't had nothin' important to say in all your life that I can remember.

More laughter and yelling.

ZUDOCK

(*portentously*)
I ordered a *house* from Sears and Roebuck!

Sounds of whistling and exclamations of disbelief.

SHERBY
What kind of a house, Zudock?

ZUDOCK
A Cape Cod Imperial. Five rooms. Comes in a kit.

The men stand stunned for a second, then almost in unison they all cheer and head for their cars. Gertz, carrying two cases of beer, stumbles but gets the beer into his car. They all head for the freight yard to see Zudock's house.

Freight yard. The men all file past the giant sleeping trains. Suddenly Zudock, who is carrying a waybill, finds his great freight car, runs up to it. His buddies help him shove open the giant sliding door. The car is crammed floor to ceiling with cardboard boxes. Big ones. The men fall back in awe.

SHERBY
Boy, there's two boxcars full of this stuff.

They help Zudock scramble up into the boxcar.

NARRATOR
A house in a kit from Sears, Roebuck! Nobody in that crowd ever owned a house. Some never even paid rent, and it was rumored that some were even squatters.

General confusion reigns as everyone tries to get into the act, unloading boxes from the car. As Zudock hands down a box, camera zooms in to red print on side of cardboard carton:

> *Warning: All items strictly coded.*
> *Check packing list carefully before opening.*

The boxes all carry enigmatic numbers: 6SJ7GT, 2311-9 (full), etc.

The celebrants heave boxes out of the boxcar, pausing now and then to refresh themselves with the beer that Gertz has so thoughtfully brought along.

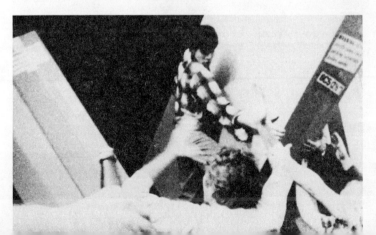

ZUDOCK

(*wrestling with box*)
Easy now, easy . . .
(*nervously, full of apprehension*)

Lots of yelling, giving of directions that nobody pays any attention to.

NARRATOR
WARNING: All items strictly coded.

The uproar continues as more and more boxes are unloaded. Somebody tips over a beer bottle which has been left on a carton, spraying Randy, who stands watching the action. Sounds of laughter interspersed with cheering, yells of encouragement.

GERTZ
Hey, I wonder what's in this one. Hey, d'ya mind if I look?

NARRATOR
Leave it to loudmouth Gertz to start the trouble.

Gertz tears open box, peers inside.

GERTZ
Well, I'll be darned. Looka that. Hey, there's windows in here. Hey, lookit. Hey, it says "attic windows."

Uncle Carl pulls open a box, stares beerily at the contents.

NARRATOR
Uncle Carl. He had a deep reef of sorrow just below the surface that came up to the top when he drank.

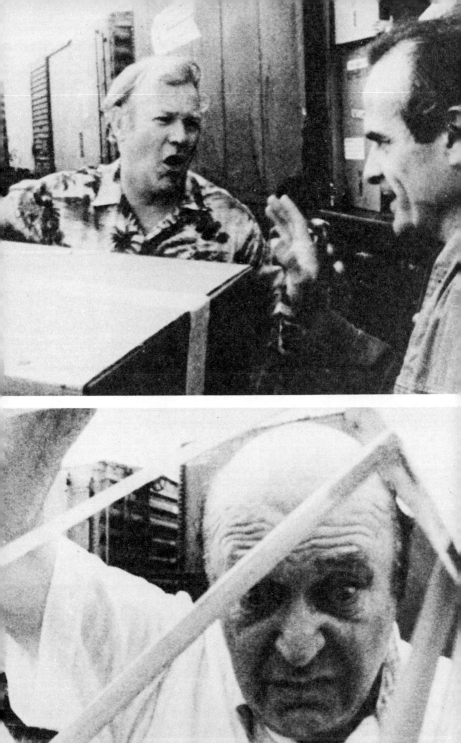

The crowd is drinking more beer as they begin to open more and more cases with more and more delight and wonderment. Uncle Carl holds up a pair of venetian blinds, true drunken wonder in his face.

UNCLE CARL
Venetian blinds . . .

The Old Man, Ralph, and Zudock are looking at Zudock's plans.

OLD MAN
Forty-nine, thirty-seven L . . .

ZUDOCK
Forty-nine, thirty seven L. Wait a minute, wait a minute. What is that?

In the background, Gertz tears open another box.

OCKIE
Hey, lookit. Hey fellas, look at what Ockie found!

He holds a toilet high over his head, amid many cheers. The party breaks out in real abandonment. Everyone is going into freight car and throwing boxes out, men are tearing open the boxes and various parts of the house are being strewn over the entire field. Someone even gets into a barrel of nails. In a few moments Zudock's house is spread over two acres. Zudock is near tears.

Gertz has climbed to the top of the boxcar. He sways alarmingly, waving beer bottle.

GERTZ

Hey, hey, heeey! Hey, everybody! Let's all hear it for Zudock's house!

Over the noise of confusion and yelling, we hear thunder rumbling. A few drops of rain spatter on Zudock's plans. He looks up in horror.

ZUDOCK

Rain? Oh no . . .

The rain becomes a downpour. The fun is over. The men leave the wreckage and begin running for their cars.

OLD MAN
(*to Zudock*)

Ya know, it's getting late. Gee, ya know, I forgot, we're going over to Bernice's house tonight. Ah, hey, Zudock, I'll see ya later. Gimme a call next week.

ZUDOCK
(*Terror . . . the worst is happening*)

Hey, wait a minute. Where ya going? Come back!

SHERBY

I'll see ya later, pal.

ZUDOCK
(*beginning to sound desperate*)

Hey, wait a minute. Where ya . . . ? Hey, hey Gertz, where ya going? Hey, come on back . . . Hey, don't leave me now.

Uncle Carl staggers past. He shrugs off Zudock's restraining hand. The rain is falling harder.

ZUDOCK
Hey come on, I gotta get this stuff outa here. Hey, HEEYYY!

NARRATOR
I'll never forget that sight as long as I live, as we pulled out of the freight yard.

Camera pulls back to reveal Zudock, a pitiful figure, alone in the rain amid the ruins of his house.

NARRATOR

(*continues*)
It was at that moment that I heard one of the most piteous cries that I've ever heard in my life.

ZUDOCK
Come baaaaaack. Hey, fellas . . . come baaack!

Cars are pulling out through the driving rain.

NARRATOR
The Old Man never looked back.

We hear "theme song" of the Phantom, Phantom's face is dimly superimposed over the departing cars.

Interior of classroom. Ralph sits at his desk, lost in a reverie.

NARRATOR
The time was growing short. I thought of Daphne all day long.

Daphne enters, long hair gently streaming over her shoulders.

NARRATOR
Daphne drifted into Biology Two, trailing mimosa blossoms and offering ecstasies not yet plumbed by human experience.

CU Daphne. Ralph can be seen behind her, mooning at her with a dumbstruck look on his face. We hear sensuous music.

Cut to teacher as she writes on blackboard, chalk screeching, ending Ralph's reverie.

Cut to back porch of house. CU of hand ringing doorbell. Mom hurries to the door.

MOM
Oh, my heavens. The Prize!

DELIVERY MAN
Where do ya want it, lady?

He struggles with enormous box.

MOM
Put it in the kitchen. Right through there. Now, be careful. Easy.

Delivery man wrestles box through screen door and into the kitchen.

MOM
Dad, your prize is here. (*To Delivery Man*) Just go right through there and put it on the table. Dad . . . do you want some help?

DELIVERY MAN
Sign here, lady.

MOM
Where? Where?

DELIVERY MAN
Right on the dotted line.

MOM
(*signing*)
Thank you very much!

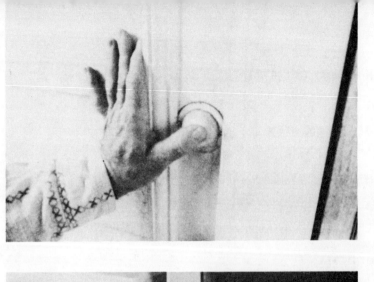

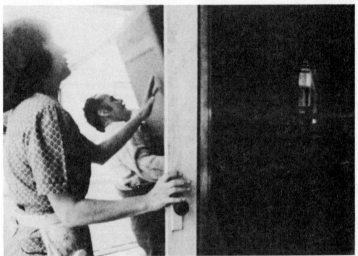

While this exchange is taking place, organ music is building up suspense in background.

DELIVERY MAN
Thanks.

He leaves. Mom, Ralph, and Randy shuffle around in the kitchen, murmuring, exclaiming over package.

The Old Man dashes in, his face flushed with excitement.

OLD MAN
Back up, back up. Don't touch it, don't touch it! Get back. Fifty grand . . . it's all in one-dollar bills.

Fumbling in supercharged haste, he searches cutlery drawer, comes up with Randy's rubber dagger, bends blade, flings it aside with exclamation of disgust, dives back into drawer, comes up with butcher knife. The organ music builds. The Old Man carefully cuts open top of box.

OLD MAN
Get back, get BACK!

As his hands dig in, a billowing mound of excelsior surges up and out. The family gathers around.

NARRATOR
The spoils of the hard-won victory. And there it was. Tenderly, he lifted from its nest of fragrant straw the only thing he had ever won in his life.

A long, white-wrapped package emerges. With infinite care the Old Man begins to peel the tissue paper from his prize. A lady's foot emerges, wearing a black high-heeled shoe. The family looks on in wonder.

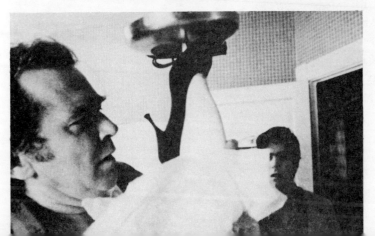

MOM
What is it?

The Old Man peels away more of the wrapping, revealing a life-size lady's leg in true blushing pink flesh tones.

OLD MAN
It's a leg. It's like . . . a statue.

MOM

(*doubtfully*)
A statue?

OLD MAN
Ohhh. Ohhhh . . . look. Would you believe it? Would you believe what this is? It's a *lamp!*

NARRATOR
We stood silent and in awe at the sheer, shimmering, unexpected beauty of the Major Award.

The Old Man plunges again into the box, hauls out a cylindrical, tissue-wrapped object.

OLD MAN
Aha! This is a lampshade.

NARRATOR
Well, naturally it was just sheer coincidence that a lady's leg was the trademark of the NeHi Company.

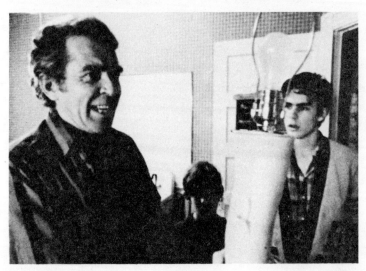

The Old Man unwraps the shade, a monstrous, barrel-shaped, bulging tube, a strident lingerie pink in color, topped by a glittering cut-crystal orb. The lamp stands a full four feet from pointed toe to sparkling crystal.

OLD MAN
This is *exactly* what we need for the front window. WOW!

He carries the lamp into the living room. The family trails behind him.

NARRATOR
The definitive lamp! A master stroke of the lightolier's art. It was without question the most magnificent lamp that we had ever seen.

OLD MAN
Get that junk off there. Where's the plug?

MOM
Behind the sofa.

Ralph is hastily removing ashtrays, plants, etc. from the table in the front window.

OLD MAN
All right, go on out into the kitchen and get me an extension cord, Fishcake.

Ralph runs into kitchen, begins to pull wires from behind the refrigerator.

NARRATOR

There were only four outlets in our house. Each one was covered with more three-way plugs and extensions than there are barnacles on the bottom of a rusting ship.

CU of Ralph's hands, trying to unsnarl a giant rat's nest of wires. He unhooks extension, runs back into living room. Ralph plugs lamp into extension, hands cord over back of sofa to the Old Man, who crouches there.

Mom flutters around, wringing her hands and making ineffectual gestures.

MOM

Now look out. There's too much on there already. You're going to get electrocuted. You remember what happened to Uncle Fred? Oh well, watch it. Ralph, you be careful too. Ralph . . . now you're gonna . . . you'd better watch it . . . you're gonna get a shock.

OLD MAN

(behind sofa)
Don't worry, I know what I'm doing.

CU fuse box as sparks fly, wires buzz and crackle.

OLD MAN
God dammit!

The lamp blazes into glowing life. Harp music is heard as it shines forth in all its translucent magnificence. The Old Man's head appears over back of sofa. His face glows with pride.

NARRATOR

It was alive! Unparalleled glory! Translucent flesh radiating a vibrant, sensual, luminous orange-yellow-pinkish nimbus of pagan fire.

The Old Man examines lamp more closely, consults tag on wire.

OLD MAN

Wait a minute. It's got two switches. (*Reading from instructions*) One is a tasteful night light, the other is an effective, scientifically designed reading lamp.

He reaches up under "skirt" of lamp to turn on other switch.

MOM

Why can't you wait until the kids are in bed?

The lamp blazes forth in full glory, pink light everywhere. We hear a harp chord.

NARRATOR

The Old Man was a full generation ahead of his time. He was the very first Pop Art fanatic.

The Old Man rushes from living room, races down front steps. He stands on the sidewalk instructing Mom in the exact positioning of the lamp.

OLD MAN

Over a little bit to the left . . . to the left . . . this way . . . more . . . ah . . . a little more . . . more . . . no, no . . . no, back.

A passing car screeches to a halt. Faces stare; fingers point.

NARRATOR
The lamp stopped traffic.

We hear the squeal of brakes.

OLD MAN
Okay, you got it. You oughta see it from out here.

Mom stands in the window, her face lighted by the lamp. She looks doubtful, almost worried.

NARRATOR
His dedication to his aesthetic principles almost wrecked our happy home.

Cut to interior of school hallway. Ralph struggles up stairs, dodging other students, trying to catch up with Daphne Bigelow.

NARRATOR
As my delicately contrived glandular system ripened and matured my juices were flowing, so my carefully concealed passion for Daphne Bigelow burgeoned until finally it engulfed me and I was swallowed up like Jonah into the inky blackness of the whale's belly of lust. Daphne Bigelow!

Ralph finally struggles through the crowd to where Daphne is removing books from her locker, her back to Ralph.

RALPH
Uh . . . Daphne . . .

Without noticing Ralph, Daphne slams locker door, turns, and hurries off to class. As she turns, we see Wanda Hickey, who has been hidden by open locker door.

WANDA

(*with her usual brightness*)
Hi, Ralph!

RALPH

(*very downcast*)
Hi.

Cut to basketball hoop. Ralph and Schwartz are playing a pick-up game on the asphalt playground. We see factories in the background, belching smoke into the air, as the boys leap and shout. Finally they decide to shoot foul shots. Ralph stands under basket, ball in hand, lining up his shot.

SCHWARTZ
How ya doin' with Daphne Bigelow?

RALPH
Well, you know, I haven't got around to asking her yet. You know.

SCHWARTZ
Ya better get on the stick.

RALPH
Hey look, don't worry about it. Who've you got lined up?

SCHWARTZ
Clara Mae Mattingly.

RALPH
(*incredulous*)
Clara Mae Mattingly?

SCHWARTZ
Yeah.

RALPH
She sure can spell.

SCHWARTZ
Sure can.

NARRATOR
It was all I could think of to say that was good about her, except, of course, that she was Female.

Schwartz is taking foul shots, missing most of them.

RALPH
Well, you gonna send her a corsage?

SCHWARTZ
I already ordered it, at the Cupid Florist.

RALPH
An orchid, right?

SCHWARTZ
It cost eight bucks.

RALPH
(*astounded*)
Eight bucks! Whew!

SCHWARTZ
(*defensive*)
Well, that includes the gold pin for it.

RALPH
Yeah, still!

Ralph and Schwartz resume shooting, shouting and yelling exuberantly.

RALPH AND SCHWARTZ
(*yelling at each other*)
Ho . . . ho . . . all right . . . hey . . . right here . . . dynamite!

Ralph's face still wears a bemused expression.

Cut to outside of steel mill. Ralph is leaving work with the rest of the shift. Steelworkers wearing their hardhats and carrying lunch pails are filing out through the gate. As Ralph goes through the gate in the steel-mesh fence, another worker catches up with him.

STEELWORKER
Hey, kid.

Ralph turns, surprised.

RALPH
Yeah?

STEELWORKER
You play third base, right?

Ralph nods yes.

STEELWORKER
I been watching. You're good. Listen, we need a third base-man for our big game. You wanna be our ringer?

RALPH
Sure, when is it?

STEELWORKER
Tuesday night at eight. Over at the church. United Brethren.

Sounds of crowd yelling.

RALPH
Won't there be some kind of problem over there? I don't go to that church.

STEELWORKER
No sweat. Listen, we got to get a team together to beat those bastards.

RALPH
Who're we playing?

STEELWORKER

(*sneering*)
Immaculate Conception.

Sounds of shouting crowd.

Cut to ball game. The stands are full and we see the teams play-ing amid the soot of the steel mills and the mosquitoes of the lake. The scene is loud and noisy. None of the speech is articu-late, just a lot of angry yelling. Tempers are running short un-der the stress of competition.

Ralph is up at bat and the first ball is a strike. Cut to lights of field, outfielders shifting their position. Lots of jeering from the competition's bench as Ralph argues with the Umpire.

NARRATOR

(over voices of the crowd)
I'd been earning ten or fifteen bucks a week playing for church teams all over town for a long time. I was a good third baseman and I could hit to the opposite field, with power.

Ralph gets a hit. The outfielders race toward each other, for the ball. Each signals "I got it"; then they collide. Ralph races around the bases.

Outfielders flail around, looking for the ball. One finds it: throws. Ralph slides into third. The infielder lays the tag on him, right in the face.

RALPH
You son of a bitch!

Cut to side angle as Ralph kicks the infielder with his left leg, knocking him over. The two ball players begin to fight, rolling over and over in the dust.

UMPIRE
All right, break it up.

Ralph and the infielder ignore him, punching and cursing. Both benches empty, and then it all breaks loose. Everybody starts fighting. The people pour out of the stands: men, women, girls, and little kids, all mixing it up in a mad melee. Dogs bark;

women scream. *We see a priest vigorously bashing someone over the head with his umbrella. CU of Immaculate Conception player getting pounded by a United Brethren stalwart. We hear sirens approaching.*

Wide cover of entire ball field covered with riot.

Sirens approach.

A nun picks her way through the melee, wringing her hands.

Sirens grow even closer.

NARRATOR
Religious wars are never ending.

Organ music is heard.

Super of Phantom's face over the insane ball-field riot.

Cut to exterior, front window of Ralph's house.

MOM

(*VO*)
I think I feel a draft.
(*Her voice cold, distant*)

Window shade is pulled down.

OLD MAN

(*VO*)
Oh, yeah? Where?

Shade goes up, revealing lamp in all its glory.

MOM

(*VO*)
I *know* I feel a draft.

Shade goes down again.

NARRATOR

(*over shot of shade*)
The breaking point at all crucial moments in history comes
stealthily, on cat feet. You never know when lightning is about
to strike, or a cornice to fall.

*Shot of movie house, marquee spelling out in white light bulbs
"Orpheum."*

NARRATOR
The Old Man's thing was bowling. And Mom had Dish Night.

Camera moves in closer to theater.

NARRATOR
The Orpheum. A tiny bastion of dreams and fantasies, a fragile
light of human aspiration in the howling darkness of the great
American Midwest. Night after night the faithful would gather,
bearing sacks of Butterfinger bars and salami sandwiches, to hud-
dle together in the darkness, staring with eyes wide with the pure
light of total belief at the flickering images. Outside those doors
crouched the pale gray wolf of Reality.

*Camera moves inside theater. We see a small figure outlined
against the screen, silhouetted by a bright white spotlight.*

DOPPLER

Ladies and gentlemen, follow along with the bouncing ball and sing along with the mighty Orpheum Wurlitzer.

Cut to screen where slide appears. Bouncing white ball begins to hop along line of lyrics as the Wurlitzer plays "I'm Forever Blowing Bubbles."

Cut to audience. We see Mom in the crowd, smiling, singing, and talking to the woman who sits next to her. She is also eating popcorn and obviously having a wonderful time.

Cut to theater lobby. Camera moves in to see light playing over tier upon tier of pearlescent, sparkling tureens, plates, saucers and gravy boats; celery holders and soup bowls. Camera moves in even closer to pick up sign proclaiming: "Free. The dinnerware of the stars."

NARRATOR

The Deluxe Pearleen Tableware. The dinner service of the stars. And all of it free. The entire town was hooked. They had the free dinnerware monkey clamped on their backs, a one-hundred-and-twelve-piece albatross growing heavier every week.

The dishes revolve slowly under the spotlight.

Ladies in the last stages of childbirth were wheeled into the Orpheum, gasping in pain, to keep the skein going. Creaking grandmothers, halt and blind, were led to the box office by grandchildren. They sat numbly, deafly, in the Orpheum seats, their watery eyes barely able to perceive the shifting, incomprehensible images on the screen but their gnarled talons clutched a gravy boat for dear life.

Mr. Doppler, like some mythical God, reigned over this, his magnetic palace of Dreams.

EVERYBODY
SING ALONG

Doppler, standing at a microphone, gestures for quiet. He holds a gravy boat in his hands. The crowd is stilled.

DOPPLER
Ladies and gentlemen, due to some unfortunate problem with the shipping, we have received the wrong piece in the magnificent set of Artistic Deluxe Pearleen Tableware, the Dinner Service of the Stars. Now I know that most of you already have a Pearleen Gravy Boat at home, but let me assure you that at next week's Dinnerware Night, we will exchange this gravy boat for a dinner plate. Thank you for your patience. And now, stand by for tonight's cartoon.

The cartoon comes on with a blast of raucous music.

Cut to a dingy hallway. Ralph and Schwartz enter, pause at cracked mirror on the wall. Ralph combs his hair.

SCHWARTZ
Some baseball game, huh, Ralph?

RALPH
Yeah, it was a . . . (*he mumbles something*) . . . Hey, here we go.

SCHWARTZ
Hey, I wonder if Fred Astaire ever comes here?

RALPH
Come on, this is serious.

BAR MITZ-
VAS, WEDDINGS,
FUNERALS and
CREMATIONS—
WE HAVE
A COSTUME
FOR EVERY—
—OCCASION.

They climb the narrow, dark wooden steps to the second floor. Within a red arrow painted on the wall are the words "swank formal—turn left." They pass a couple of dentists' offices and a door marked "bail bondsman—freedom for you day or night." A smaller hand-lettered sign on the door reads "closed."

Ralph and Schwartz enter Al's Swank Formalwear. It is a small tacky room with a yellow light bulb hanging from the ceiling, a couple of tall glass cases containing suits on hangers, a counter, and a couple of smudgy full-length mirrors. A swarthy, bald, hawk-eyed, shirt-sleeved man is standing behind the counter. Around his neck hangs a yellow measuring tape. He wears a worn vest with a half-dozen chalk pencils sticking out of the pocket.

SCHWARTZ
Uh . . . we'd like to . . . uh . . .

AL
(*expansively*)
Okay boys, you wanna make a big hit at the Prom, hah? Ya goin' to that hop at Cherrywood, am I right? (**RALPH** *and* **SCHWARTZ** *mumble "Yeah"*) And you want some summah formals, right?

(*Again the boys nod*)
I know, I know. (*Shouts*) *Morty!*

MORTY
(*from behind him*)
I'm here.

AL
Oh.

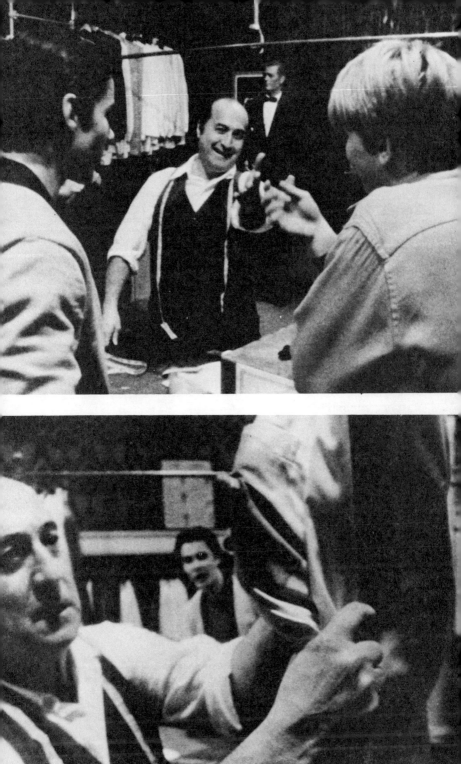

MORTY
Whadda ya want?

AL
Look, we got a coupla new customers for that bash at Cherry-wood.

MORTY
Yeah, yeah.

Morty, a tall, thin, sad man in a gray smock, carries two suits on hangers, drapes them over the counter, gives Al a dirty look, and stalks back into the shadows.

AL
(*calls after him*)
I would say a thirty-six short . . .

MORTY *mumbles "Yeah, yeah."*

AL
. . . and a *fawty regulah.*

MORTY
(*from far away*)
Comin' up.

Humming to himself, Al begins to pile and unpile boxes as if Schwartz and Ralph were not even there.

MORTY
(*from the bowels of the establishment*)
Hey Al, okay on the thirty-six short, but I'm out of the forties. How about that forty-two regulah that just came back from the Dago wedding?

AL
Cut the talk and bring it awready!

MORTY
But the forty-two regulah ain't been cleaned yet!

AL
(*shouting*)
BRING IT OUT AWREADY!

Al smiles sunnily at the boys. From the back room we hear the sound of boxes falling.

AL
Ya see, this . . . ah . . . this suit just came from anotha job, ya see. But don't worry. We'll clean it up, we'll fit it to ya, and it'll look just as good as new.

Morty emerges with two summer formals, hangs them on pipe rack next to the counter, disappears again into the back room. Al grabs a suit, shoves it at Schwartz.

AL
I'll tell you what. Here, you, you first. C'mere. Here, here take this, take this, c'mon, come wit me, here now, back here there's a dressin' room. Go behind the curtain and try . . . try it . . . try the pants on.

He propels Schwartz toward the back.
(*calling after Schwartz*) Lissen, if it's too long in the cuffs, don't worry about it, we'll take it up.

Al turns to Ralph.

AL
Now you.

Al holds up the other suit. In the middle of a dark reddish-brown stain which covers the entire right breast pocket is a sinister little hole, right through the jacket. Al turns the hanger around and sticks his finger through the hole.

AL
I got . . . ah . . . (*he gives embarrassed chuckle*) . . . *Morty!*

Morty emerges, scowling.
Morty, Morty, one question, about this hole in this regulah forty-two. Can ya fix it?

MORTY
Whadda ya want, miracles?

Al gives another chuckle, grabs Ralph, shoves suit into his hands.

AL
Kid! C'mere, step over here. Lissen, don't worry about the coat. We'll clean it up, it'll be as good as new. You'll never know that this wasn't a new coat.

Ralph, too, is propelled into the rear of the store.

AL
Here, hold that. (*To Schwartz*) Hey you, come on out, I wanna take a look at you.

SCHWARTZ
(*from behind curtain*)
I ain't got my pants on yet!

AL
Come on out, you're among friends. Step out here.

Schwartz emerges from the fitting room shrouded in what looks like a parachute with sleeves.

AL
Beyoootiful. Look at that. Looks like it was made for you.

He measures Schwartz quickly and roughly, hands coat to Ralph.

AL
Slip into tha . . . easy now, it's a very delicate material.

Ralph puts on coat. Stain goes from top of breast pocket half-way to his navel.

AL
There you are. (*Rapturously*) Oh, perfect! Oh, bettah than the othah one. Look at that fit, it's beyootiful, and looka this here. Look how tight it is in the back. Oh, it fits ya like a glove. I wish your mother were here to see this fit, it's beyootiful. The shoulders are . . . it's wonderful . . . Look, we'll take it in a little here . . .

He helps Ralph off with coat, sticks his finger through hole again.

AL

Boy, that musta been some party. (*Chuckles*)

Schwartz emerges again, wearing suit pants. They are about three feet too long.

Good, the pants look good.

They return to the counter.

AL

Now, that'll be twenty dollars apiece deposit. Twenty from you, and twenty from the small gentleman here.

Ralph gives Al twenty-dollar bill; Schwartz looks upset.

SCHWARTZ

I only got sixteen.

RALPH

(*whispering, embarrassed*)

Schwartz! I thought you had twenty.

SCHWARTZ

I went to the soda shop . . .

AL

Well, fellas . . .

RALPH

Schwartz, I thought you had twenty dollars.

AL

I'll tell ya what. Such high-class customers, fifteen dollars apiece deposit from each one of ya, okay?

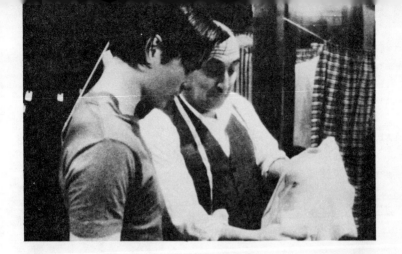

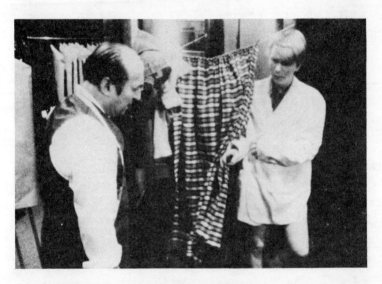

SCHWARTZ
Thank you . . .

AL
Now don't . . . don't thank me. And above all don't tell my partner.

Al gives them a conspiratorial wink, glances toward back room as if expecting to see Morty come out raging with protest.

RALPH AND SCHWARTZ
No, no, we won't.

AL
Now I'll wrap everything and have it ready for ya for the Prom.

He winks again.

AL
Lemme tell ya, two high-class customers like you, you'll knock 'em dead!

Cut to interior Ralph's house. Ralph enters, walks through the house, preoccupied. He passes his mother, who is dusting in the living room.

NARRATOR
A softness was in the air.

The Old Man is in the shower.

OLD MAN
(*off camera*)
Hey, HEY!

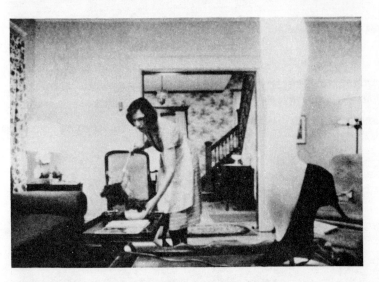

NARRATOR

A quickening of the pulse.

OLD MAN

Hey, HEY! What happened to the water pressure? Who's foolin' around?

NARRATOR

Expectation long lying dormant in the blackened rock ice of winter . . .

OLD MAN

Ahhh, that's better. (*Begins to sing lustily*)

Ralph goes into kitchen, looks in refrigerator, takes out pop bottle. Randy sits at kitchen table.

NARRATOR

. . . sent out tentative, tender green shoots and yawned toward the smoky sun. Somewhere off in the distance, ball met bat, robin called to robin, and a screen door slammed.

We hear Mom humming to herself as she dusts.

NARRATOR

One week to go. My cowardly soul, could I ever ask Daphne Bigelow . . .

SFX

CRAAASSHH!
FREEZE FRAME: *Ralph's face, horrified.*
                Randy, likewise.
                The Old Man, covered with shaving
                cream, face frozen in fear and disbelief.

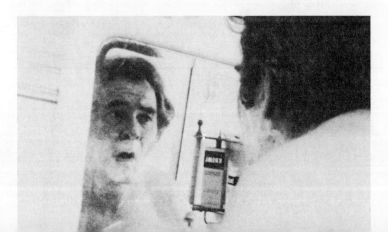

Cut to outside of house. Over shot of house we hear the Old Man's voice.

OLD MAN

What broke? What happened? WHAT BROKE?!

Cut to living room. The Old Man rushes in, face covered with shaving cream, eyes rolling wildly.

OLD MAN

What broke? What broke? (*Piteously*) Oh, my lamp, my lamp!

CU of shattered kneecap under the coffee table, the cracked, well-turned ankle under the radio, the calf split, its wire hanging out limply over the rug. The Old Man crouches over the wreckage.

OLD MAN

Oh, my lamp. You broke it. (*Angrily*) My lamp!

MOM

I don't know what happened. I was just dusting and . . .

OLD MAN

You broke my lamp because you're jealous!

MOM

Jealous! Of a plastic leg?

OLD MAN
(*bitterly*)
You're jealous because I *won*.

MOM
(*guiltily*)
That's ridiculous. Jea-jeal-jealous of what?

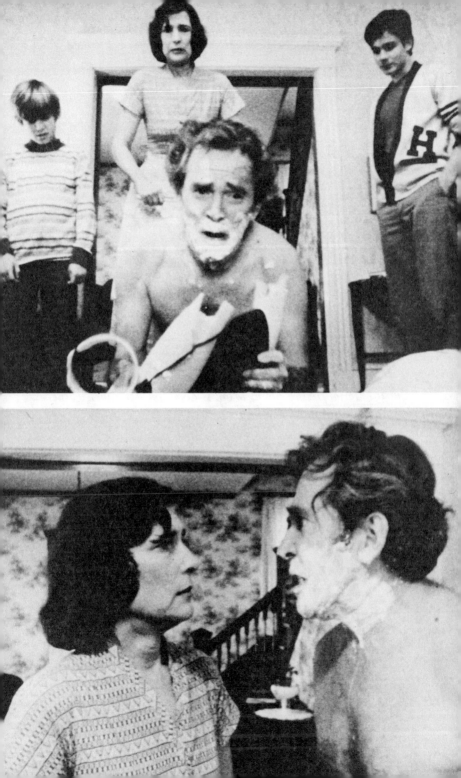

OLD MAN
(*grimly*)
Get the glue.

MOM
We're out of glue.

OLD MAN
DAMMIT!

The Old Man charges up the stairs, disappears into bedroom, slamming the door. Almost instantly he charges back out. Ralph goes to the window. Old Man gets in car and slams the door of his Oldsmobile. The window falls out and smashes. Car is shoved into reverse. The fender drags along the edge of the garage. Finally car roars off down the street.

Cut to interior, living room. Mom is down on her knees, gathering up pieces of smashed lamp.

NARRATOR
Quietly, my mother started picking up the pieces, something she did all her life.

Ralph wanders outside. He picks up the hose that's lying there and starts to sprinkle the lawn.

The Old Man's car comes screeching into the yard, and the Old Man rushes into the house.

NARRATOR
You could always tell the mood of the Old Man by the way he drove. Today there was no question.

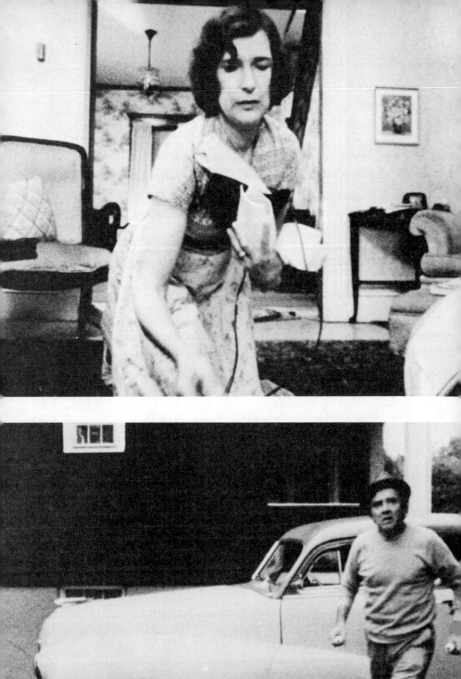

OLD MAN
(*charging up back stairs*)
Don't touch that lamp!

NARRATOR
He's carrying glue, *iron* glue. The kind that garage mechanics used for gaskets and for gluing back together exploded locomotives.

Ralph stands on the lawn, moodily sprinkling the grass, his mind a million miles away. From inside the house we hear the Old Man swearing as he struggles with pieces of the lamp.

WANDA
What're you doing?

Startled, Ralph flings the hose around, spraying the white figure on the sidewalk ten feet away, dressed in tennis garb. Wanda shrieks.

RALPH
Sorry. I didn't . . .

Wanda squeals as he inadvertently sprays her again.

WANDA
Ralph!

RALPH
Sorry. I . . . I didn't . . .

Cut to inside of house. The Old Man sits at the kitchen table, trying desperately to glue back together his precious lamp.

Cut back to outside of house, Ralph and Wanda on lawn.

RALPH
You been playing tennis?
(*He is barely listening to her through entire scene*)

WANDA
Me and Eileen Akers were playing down at the park.

She sits on picnic table, holding her tennis racket. Ralph sits on bench.

WANDA
I'm glad school's almost over. I can hardly wait. I never thought I'd be a senior.

RALPH
(*absently*)
Yeah, I know.

WANDA
I'm going to camp this summer. Are you?

RALPH
Nah.

Cut to inside the house. The Old Man almost gets the leg together when the kneecap springs off and sails across the kitchen.

Cut back to outside, Ralph and Wanda.

WANDA
Are you gonna go to college when you graduate next year?

RALPH
I dunno. I guess so, if I don't get drafted or anything.

WANDA

My brother's in the Army. He's in the artillery.

RALPH

Yeah, I heard. Does he like it much?

Wanda shrugs.

WANDA

He doesn't write much. He's gonna get a pass next September before he goes overseas.

RALPH

How come he's in the artillery?

WANDA

I don't know. They just put him there. I guess because he's tall.

RALPH

(*incredulous*)

He's *tall?* What does that have to do with it? Does he have to throw the shells or something?

WANDA

I don't know. They just did it.

Cut back to kitchen. The Old Man struggles with lamp.

OLD MAN

Now I gotcha, now I gotcha . . . ahhh!

His elbow hits foot; it falls off kitchen table.

Cut back to lawn, Ralph and Wanda.

RALPH

(*after moment of hesitation*)
So . . . you going to the Prom?

For a long instant Wanda says nothing, just swings her tennis racket in the air.

WANDA

(*weakly*)
I guess so.

RALPH
It's gonna be pretty good, huh?

WANDA
Yeah. Uh . . . who're you going with?

RALPH
Well, I haven't made up my mind yet.

Ralph bends down unconcernedly and pulls a blade of grass out by the roots.

WANDA
Neither have I.

They look at each other, frozen in time.

NARRATOR

It was then that I realized there was no sense fighting it.

Quick shot of Daphne, swinging on a swing, her long dress blowing, her hair floating out behind her.

NARRATOR

Some guys are born to dance forever with the Daphne Bigelows, on shining ballroom floors under endless starry skies.

Another quick shot of the beautiful Daphne.

NARRATOR

Others? Well, they do the best they can.

RALPH

Wanda . . .

WANDA

Yeah?

RALPH

Well, I was thinking . . .

Cut to kitchen. The Old Man, still fighting the lamp, has glue all over the place.

Cut to outside.

WANDA
Yeah?

RALPH
I uh . . . I was thinking that . . . well, maybe that . . .

Quick cut to Daphne on swing.

RALPH

. . . that uh . . . well, uh . . .

Another quick cut to Daphne.

RALPH

(*in a rush*)
Ya wanna go to the Prom with me?

Cut to empty swing, forlornly losing speed, slowing, slowing.

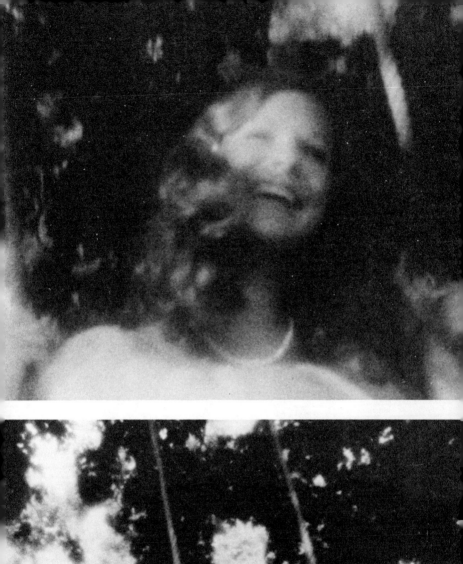

Cut to inside of kitchen. The Old Man angrily scoops all the pieces of lamp from the table, storms outside, and dumps them into the garbage can.

WANDA

Of course! . . . I've had several invitations but I haven't said yes to any of them yet. It'd be fun to go with you. I guess.

RALPH
(resigned to his fate)
Well, ya know, I have had several girls that wanted to go with me but ha, well, I figured they were mostly jerks anyway and, well, I wanted to ask you all along, ya know.

Slowly camera pulls back and up, leaving Ralph and Wanda as smaller and smaller figures as they slowly begin to walk up the street. The sun has about set and already the steel mills have begun to reflect their glow in the evening sky.

NARRATOR

The die was cast. There was no turning back. The great Atlantic salmon struggling thousands of miles upstream, leaping water-falls, battling bears to mate is nothing compared to your average high school junior. The salmon dies in the attempt, and so, often, does the junior, in more ways than one. As we ambled on through the gloom, I didn't have the slightest hint of what was coming. Neither, I suppose, does the salmon. He just does what he has to do. So did I.

Scene slowly fades.

Cut to the kitchen sink, gurgling throatily.

NARRATOR

The battle at home had moved into the trench warfare or Great Freeze stage.

Pull back to see Mom removing apron, taking purse from hook on kitchen wall. The Old Man sits at table, reading newspaper.

MOM
Randy, please tell your father that I am going to the Orpheum.

RANDY
Dad, Mom's going to the Orpheum.

OLD MAN
Hmmph.

MOM
I'll be back . . . you're to go to bed at eight-thirty. Now I mean it! I'll be back as soon as I have traded in these two gravy boats for the Deluxe dinner plate and the Deluxe sugar bowl.

RANDY
Can you bring me some ice cream home, Mom? Please? Pleeze?

MOM
We'll see.

Mom leaves. She closes door and camera zooms in on the Old Man, who is still reading paper. Headline reads "White Sox Lose Six In A Row."

NARRATOR
All communications had ceased between the warring parties. There was only the sink for company.

Cut to CU of sink, which makes long, gurgling sound.

Cut to the stage of the Orpheum and a white screen. Doppler stands next to a huge wheel which slowly turns as the audience watches in suspense.

NARRATOR
Dish Night, Sing-Alongs, Talent contests and, yes, Screeno, were all part of Doppler's vast sonata of entertainment. He offered everything except decent movies.

The mighty Orpheum Wurlitzer is playing through this.

The wheel slowly stops. The crowd gasps. The wheel turns backward slowly, slowly, drawing another gasp from the crowd.

CU of wheel as it tick tick ticks; finally stops.

DOPPLER
Red twenty-eight.

A lady in the crowd leaps excitedly to her feet.

LADY
Screeno!

Camera pulls back to see Doppler standing next to large paper sack of groceries.

DOPPLER
And now for the grand prize of the evening, five dollars' worth of groceries from the Piggly-Wiggly store on Calumet Avenue. Credit Extended, Superb Meat and Groceries, We Cash Checks. Come back to my office right after the feature to win your grand prize. About the gravy boats . . .

An ugly mutter runs through the crowd.

NARRATOR
Doppler booted it again. The fourth gravy boat in a row.

Cut to high school.

Ralph and Schwartz are at school, hurrying through the halls between classes on their way to their lockers.

VOICE OVER LOUDSPEAKER
Prom tickets to the dance must be picked up today in Mrs. Munson's office. The tickets must be picked up by three o'clock.

RALPH
Hey, hey Schwartz, c'mere. You're gonna go with me to the Prom, on a double date, right?

SCHWARTZ
Great! I'll help you clean your car.

RALPH
No, no listen. I already fixed it. Split the gas, all right?

SCHWARTZ
You gonna send Daphne an orchid or what?

RALPH
Ah . . . no . . . I'm not.

SCHWARTZ
Whatta ya mean? Ya gotta send her a corsage.

RALPH
I am. I'm sending a corsage. What are you talking about?

SCHWARTZ
You just said you weren't.

RALPH

Hey, I never said I wasn't gonna send a corsage.

SCHWARTZ

You nut, you just said you weren't gonna . . .

RALPH

Hey, dummy, I just said I wasn't gonna send *Daphne* a corsage, awright? I'm not.

SCHWARTZ

She's gonna think you're a real cheapskate.

RALPH

Hey, I'm not gonna take Daphne to the Prom, ya understand? I'm takin' Wanda Hickey.

Schwartz stops and looks directly at Ralph, causing him to slam into two strolling freshmen girls. Their books slide across the floor, where they are trampled underfoot by the thundering mob. Ralph pushes through the door to the stairway. Schwartz follows.

SCHWARTZ

Wanda Hickey? Wanda *Hickey?*

RALPH

(*defiantly*)
Yeah, Wanda Hickey.

SCHWARTZ
Well, she sure is good in algebra.

Dissolve to shot of study hall. It is afternoon and Ralph is seated at one of the tables. His study books are open, but he is staring absently across the room at Wanda who, unaware of him, is busily at work.

NARRATOR
Wanda Hickey! Look at those stupid glasses! That hair! And I was taking Wanda Hickey—Wanda Hickey, of all people!—to the Prom, the only Junior Prom of my life!

(*Small sob*)

Ralph begins busily figuring in his notebook.

RALPH
(*to himself*)
Let's see, eight dollars for the orchid, and half the gas . . . a dollar, and ah, ten dollars for the formal . . .

Ralph straightens up with a little exclamation of despair. CU sheet of notebook paper; Ralph's figures.

RALPH
(*aloud*)
Oh no, six dollars. Uh oh!

We see that after his expenses, Ralph will have a big six dollars to squander on the Prom.

From behind Ralph, Schwartz gets up, casually walks past as if on his way to the john. He tosses note onto Ralph's deck. CU note: "How about the Red Rooster afterward?"

Ralph takes the piece of paper and writes "Where else?" and passes it back to Schwartz.

NARRATOR
The Red Rooster was part of the tribal ritual. It was the place you went after a big date, if you could afford it.

Ralph glances over across the room at Wanda again.

NARRATOR
Wanda Hickey. Yuuck, what a drag.

Cut to kitchen. Ralph is seated at the table, eating a liverwurst sandwich and drinking a glass of milk. It is nighttime. The back door slams open and the Old Man enters, carrying his bowling bag. He slides the bag across the floor, pretending to lay one down the groove, his right arm held out in a graceful follow-through, right leg training in the classic bowling stance.

OLD MAN
Right in the pocket!

RALPH
How'd you do tonight?

OLD MAN
Not bad, not bad. Had a two-oh-seven game. Almost broke six hundred.

RALPH

(*admiringly*)
Ahh.

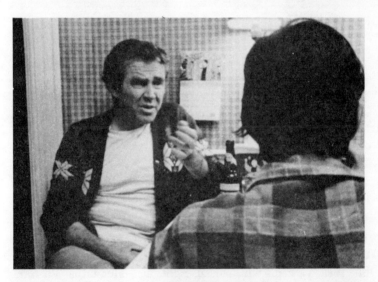

The Old Man opens the refrigerator. A head of lettuce falls out. He fields it on the first bounce, returns it to refrigerator, removes a beer, stands beside the sink, taking a deep drag from the bottle and burping loudly.

OLD MAN
Had a five-eighty-seven series. And that was in lane eight, which is a very bad lane.

He sits down at table.

OLD MAN
Well, tomorrow's the big night, ain't it?

RALPH
Yeah, it sure is.

OLD MAN
You takin' ah Daphne . . . Bigelow?

RALPH
(*a bit downcast*)
Nah, I'm takin' Wanda Hickey.

OLD MAN
Ohh. Well, ya can't win 'em all, right, kid? Her father's a fore-man of some kind or somethin' at the mill, ain't he?

RALPH
Yeah, something like that.

OLD MAN
He drives a Studebaker Champion, green, two-door, whitewalls. Not a bad car. Except it burns oil after a while. Some of 'em have a very bad front end. Rotten kingpins.

The Old Man shakes his head critically, opens another beer and reaches for the rye bread.

OLD MAN
How ya fixed for the dance?

RALPH
What do you mean?

OLD MAN
I mean how ya fixed?

RALPH
I got six bucks.

There is silence for a minute or two. They chew on their sandwiches.

OLD MAN
(*thoughtfully*)
I sure wish I coulda gone to one a them Proms. Oh well, what the hell. Hey, listen, I was really hot tonight. Got six straight strikes. The old hook was really movin', hittin' a lot of wood.

He reaches into his hip pocket, takes out his wallet.

OLD MAN
(*leans forward, conspiratorially*)
Don't tell your mother. I made a coupla bets on the second game, and I'm a money bowler.

He lays a twenty-dollar bill on the table.

Ralph smiles. They both continue to eat their sandwiches, looking at each other but saying nothing.

Camera pans along Ralph's bed where can be seen his entire summer formal ensemble laid out.

NARRATOR
Old Al and Morty had really come through. Look at that coat. Looks great! Cary Grant would be proud to wear it. That shirt, ohh, it's so stiff it creaks. It was just getting to be twilight when I emerged from the bathroom, redolent of dynamic Aqua Velva. It was Prom night at last.

Ralph begins to get dressed. He struggles to fasten the tight collar of the shirt. Randy sticks his head in the door, pantomimes strangulation.

RANDY
Gaaaak!

Mom comes in; helps Ralph on with his white formal coat. Ralph dashes into bathroom; Mom follows.

MOM
Ohh, Ralph, what is this thing called?

She has something in her hand. Ralph looks.

RALPH
What?

MOM
This.

RALPH
Oh, that's my boutonniere. It's like a fake flower.
Ralph turns to leave.

MOM
Now don't leave before I get dressed. I want to see you.

She is wearing her rump-sprung red chenille bathrobe, with the petrified egg on the lapel. And one side of her hair is rolled up on little aluminum rheostats.

RALPH
Okay.

Cut to stairway. Ralph comes running down, followed by Mom who is now dressed. Ralph rushes around, making a last-minute check of his clothes, etc.

RALPH
(*to himself*)
Keys . . .

MOM
Gosh, you look nice. Now have you got everything?

RALPH
Yes, Ma.

MOM
A handkerchief?

RALPH
Yes, Ma.

MOM
A comb?

RALPH

Listen, Ma, I'm not a kid. Will ya just let me go? I'll be back late. Don't wait up.

MOM

Oh, your corsage, Ralph!

Ralph rushes into kitchen, rushes back out with florist's cardboard box.

MOM

Oh, Ralph, wait. I want to take a picture!

RALPH

Not now!

MOM

Come on.

She is pushing him up against the stairway, fumbling with camera. Ralph looks disgusted.

RALPH

No. Oh, *Ma.*

MOM

Your Aunt Clara will love this. You're gonna treasure it, Ralph. All right, now don't squint. Smile, dear.

Mom snaps picture.

Quick cut to snapshot of Ralph in his formal coat. It is a typical "Mother" picture, badly composed and slightly out of focus.

NARRATOR

Believe it or not, I've still got that picture. Everybody in America's got a Prom picture, stuck away somewhere they never show to anyone and for good reason.

Shots of Ralph leaving house, getting into car and driving to pick up Wanda. He pulls up at house, and instantly Wanda is out of the door and waiting for him on the porch. Ralph gets out of car and slowly walks up path to meet her. Ralph reaches Wanda. Wanda is wearing a long turquoise taffeta gown, her milky skin and dark hair radiating in the glow of the porch light.

NARRATOR

This was not the same old Wanda. She didn't have her glasses on, and her eyes were unnaturally large and liquid, the way the true myopia victim's always are.

RALPH

Hi.

WANDA

Hi.

RALPH

You look great. This is for you.

Ralph hands her florist box. Wanda peeks inside.

WANDA

Oh gee, thanks for the orchid.

RALPH
Let's go.

WANDA
Okay.

Ralph and Wanda enter car and drive off down the road.

RALPH
It's gonna be great. They got this great band.

NARRATOR
In accordance with tribal custom, she, too, was being mercilessly clamped by straps and girdles and hooks.

RALPH
Glad the weather's gonna be good. It's a kind of nice night out. Great night for a Prom.

WANDA
Yeah.

Dissolve to car pulling up in front of Clara Mae's house. Clara Mae and Schwartz jump in. Car roars off.

RALPH
Come on, let's go, ho!

CLARA MAE
Hi, Wanda.

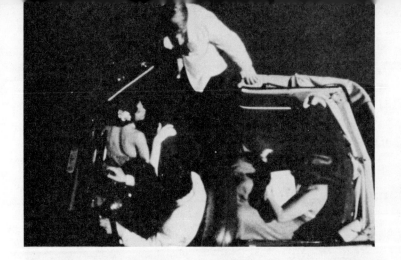

WANDA
Hi, how are you?

RALPH

(*shouting over his shoulder*)
Hey, Schwartz, what time you gotta be in?

SCHWARTZ

(*laughing*)
Oh, I don't have to be in any time.

RALPH
All *right!*

SCHWARTZ
I can't wait till we take on the Red Rooster!

RALPH
I know, I know!

Dissolve to shot of parking lot in front of Cherrywood Country Club as streams of cars pull in. We see Ralph and friends park, jump out of car, and thread their way through the crowd and into the club.

NARRATOR

Oh-ho, the Prom was going full blast when we made our dramatic entrance. Everybody was there. I found myself saying things like "Why, hello there, Albert, how are you?" and "Why yes, I believe the weather is perfect."

Camera pulls back to reveal entire dance floor.

Mickey Eisley and his Magic Music Makers struck up the sultry sounds that had made them famous in every steel-mill town that ringed Lake Michigan. Dark and sensuous the dance floor engulfed all of us. I felt tall and slim. I could see myself standing on a mysterious balcony, looking out over the lights of some distant, exotic city.

CU Wanda's face as she dreamily dances with Ralph.

Quick cut to Daphne, beautiful long hair flowing as she skips along a beach.

CU Wanda's face.

CU Flick (in scene from hamburger joint)

FLICK

(*voice echoes*)
Who ya takin'?

Another quick shot of Daphne.

OLD MAN'S VOICE
Ya takin' ah Daphne Bigelow?

CU Wanda.

CU Flick.

FLICK
Who ya takin'?

CU Daphne.

SCHWARTZ'S VOICE

(*echoing*)
Wanda Hickey? You're taking *Wanda Hickey* to the Prom?

Dance music fades and is replaced by very romantic, dramatic melody. Suddenly Daphne, the real Daphne, is there on the dance floor. She wears a long white gown and her hair is highlighted with a sparkling diamond tiara. She dances, sweeping around the floor, with a tall, slender young man in a black tuxedo. They look rather like Ginger Rogers and Fred Astaire amid the shuffling herd of lumpy kids. Ralph's eyes follow her yearningly as she sweeps past with her handsome partner.

RALPH
Hi, Daphne.

DAPHNE

(*absently*)
Hi, Howard.

She whirls away on the arm of her partner.

NARRATOR
Ah, Daphne. Nothing ever quite works out.

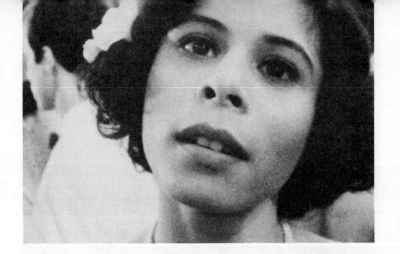

Cut to house. Sitting apart, not talking, Mom and the Old Man sit in living room. Mom is sewing a frayed elbow in Randy's sweater and the Old Man is still reading the paper. It's the great freeze. Cut back and forth between the two, each holding out waiting for the other one to speak. At last . . .

OLD MAN
You know . . .

Mom straightens up and waits.
. . . I like the room this way.

She looks down again at her darning and in a soft voice . . .

MOM
Uh . . . you know, I'm . . . I'm sorry I broke it.

OLD MAN

(*expansive*)
Ahh . . . it was really pretty jazzy.

MOM
No, I thought it was very . . . pretty.

OLD MAN
Nah. It was too pink for this room. What that front window needs is a nice brass lamp.

Mom continues darning. Then the Old Man drops the funnies noisily to get her attention.

144

OLD MAN

What do you say we all go to the movies, huh? You wanna go to the movies?

Mom looks up in surprise.

MOM

But this is Dish Night. You never go to the movies on Dish Night. Ah . . . they're giving away the Deluxe Hollywood bun warmer.

OLD MAN

It's still the movies, right? (*He looks perplexed*) What the hell's a bun warmer?

MOM

Well, I don't know, but *Woman's Home Companion* says that Loretta Young uses one.

OLD MAN

Randy, Randy, get dressed. We're goin' to the movies!

Cut back to the country club. A tune has ended and Ralph heads for the punch bowl, leaving Wanda sitting with Clara Mae. Schwartz, too, is getting punch for his date.

SCHWARTZ
Hey, Ralph.

RALPH
How ya doin', Schwartz?

They are joined by Flick.

FLICK

(*to Ralph*)
Heeyy, I couldn't believe it, man. I almost flipped when I heard you were bringin' Wanda to the Prom.

RALPH
Yeah, well, I'm not the only one here with a dog.

SCHWARTZ
That Clara Mae's hair smells just like a cheese Danish, I swear.

FLICK
Yeah, ha ha.

RALPH
Hey, you got no movie star either.

FLICK
Ahh, she's no date, she's my cousin. Cousin's not an actual girl.

RALPH
Talk about me slippin'. Hey, you see that guy who's with Daphne?

SCHWARTZ
They say they flew him all the way from Princeton just to be at the dance.

(*Exclamations from the other two*)

SCHWARTZ
He's even going *bald!*

FLICK
Ah, Bruner says he's goin' to law school.

(*More exclamations*)

RALPH
Hey, listen, get out your leashes, guys. We gotta go walk the dogs.

Cut back to bandstand. A hush descends on the dance floor as Mickey Eisley, standing in a baby spot before a microphone shaped like a chromium bullet, announces in a metallic voice ringing with feedback.

MICKEY EISLEY
All right, gang, and now for something romantic. We have a request for "Stahdust" and for this one we're going to turn down the lights.

The lights fade even lower. Only the Japanese lanterns glow dimly—red, green, yellow, and blue—in the enchanted darkness.

Wanda and Ralph begin to maneuver around the floor.

NARRATOR
Wanda started to sweat through her taffeta. I felt it running down her back. My own back was so wet you could read the label on my T-shirt right through the dinner jacket. So that she wouldn't notice, I pulled Wanda closer to me.

CU Ralph's hand on Wanda's back.
I felt bumpy things under her gown, little hooks and knobs, little round things. Sighing, she hugged me back.

Cut to Flick, doing some sort of wild gyrations amid the shuffling dancers.
Good old Flick was doing his thing with his lumpy cousin.

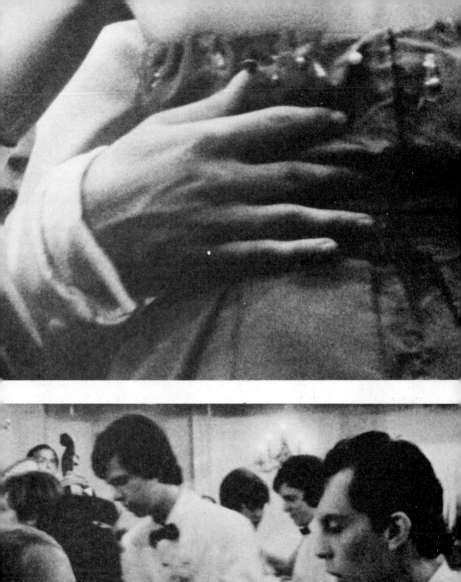
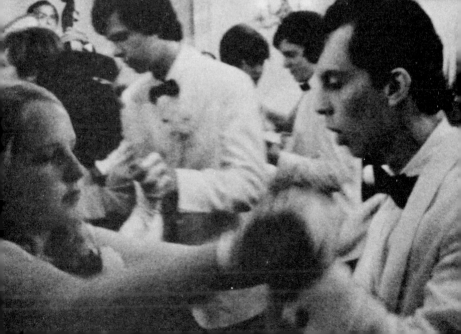

CU Wanda's orchid.
Wanda's orchid was leering up at me from her shoulder. It was the most repulsive flower I had ever seen. It looked like some kind of overgrown Venus flytrap waiting for the right moment to strike.

Camera pulls in even closer to orchid.
Deep purple, with an obscene yellow tongue that stuck straight out of it, and greenish knobs on the end. It clashed almost audibly with her turquoise dress. It looked like it was *breathing!*

Music ends. Wanda smiles up dreamily at Ralph.

Cut to ticket booth at Orpheum, POV ticket-taker. Mom, Old Man, and Randy reach head of line.

MOM
Could I have two adults and one child, please? Thank you.

Cut to inside the lobby. An usher stands, eyes downcast, handing out yet another gravy boat. He hands one to Mom.

MOM
I don't . . .

USHER
That's okay, you can speak to Mr. Doppler.

He hands gravy boat to the Old Man.
Sorry, sir.

Mom, the Old Man, and Randy enter the theater auditorium. On this night no gay music played through the theater loud-speakers. No coming attractions. There is no sound except for the angry clanking of gravy boats.

Mr. Doppler, looking terrified, stands in the wings.

A sudden blinding spotlight hits the maroon curtain, next to the cold, silent screen, and out of the wings, Mr. Doppler appears.

DOPPLER
Ah . . . ladies, I have to apologize for tonight's gravy boat.

Angry rattle of china.
I personally guarantee you that *next* week . . .

The audience starts a low hissing sound.

Next week . . . (*Doppler continues bravely*) I personally guarantee that we will exchange all gravy boats for . . .

SFX of a whistling object.

A dark shadow, slow motion, slices through the beam of the spotlight, casting an enormous shadow of a great gravy boat on the screen. Spinning over and over, it crashes on the stage at Doppler's feet.

DOPPLER

(*leaping out of the way*)
Ladies, please!

Instantly a blizzard of gravy boats fills the air.
Now, ladies and gentlemen . . . !

Doppler leaps desperately about the stage, dodging gravy boats.

Dissolve to shot of Ralph continuing the dance. Orchestra is playing, and the bass player is now singing "Good Night, Sweetheart." Wanda clings to Ralph, gazing up at him dreamily.

Cut back to Orpheum. Gravy boats continue to be hurled at the stage. Doppler desperately signals "Start the film!" And the screen is suddenly filled with whooping Indians brandishing rifles. The theater roars with gunfire, the thunder of hoofs, the crash of gravy boats.

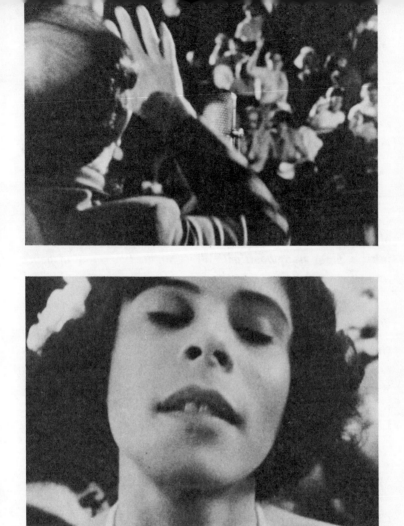

Cut back to dance. "Good Night, Sweetheart" has reached its most syrupy stages, and the bass player is giving it his all. Wanda moons romantically up at Ralph.

Cut back to Orpheum. Gravy boats sail through the air in a beautiful slow-motion ballet.

Camera cuts back to dance. More "Good Night, Sweetheart."

Cut back to Orpheum. The cavalry is now arriving, in a blast of trumpets and gunfire. The audience, jumping up and down in rage, flings gravy boats with all its might. The sound of police sirens pierces the din.

Cut to outside of Orpheum. Crowd mills around on the sidewalk under the marquee as the sirens grow louder and louder.

Cut to exterior of Cherrywood Country Club. Ralph stands under the portico, looking out at a torrential downpour.

NARRATOR
Look at it come down. Ohh . . .

Ralph pulls coat up over his head, dashes for the parking lot.
Must be six foot deep there under my hubcaps.

CU of car door being opened. Water cascades out.

NARRATOR
Oh no! Why the hell did I leave my top down!

Ralph tries to raise the convertible top by pushing the button. The canopy raises halfway and jams. Cursing, with rain pouring down his face, his hair matted in front of his eyes, Ralph continues to pound the relay button. Finally he stands up and hauls at the top with all his strength.

NARRATOR
Do you know what happens to a maroon wool carnation on a white coat in a heavy June downpour in the Midwest, where it rains not water but carbolic acid from the steel-mill fallout?

Drenched, Ralph struggles with top.

RALPH
Come on!

NARRATOR
This never happened to Fred Astaire. And if it rained on Gene Kelly, he just sang and danced on the street, and it was Paris.

Top finally raises. Ralph grinds the starter feebly. At last it catches, and the engine starts.

Cut to front of Cherrywood Country Club. Schwartz, Wanda, and Clara Mae pile into car.

NARRATOR
Our merry band headed for the Red Rooster. The adolescent tribal rite of the Prom was nearing its final and most vicious phase.

Car moves forward in a series of feeble lurches.

Cut to large sign on easel, done in silver glitter on a red and blue background: "The Red Rooster proudly presents in our Aquarium Lounge—the lovely Arlita."

Cut to interior of Red Rooster. Ralph guides Wanda through the uproarious throng of his peers. Schwartz and Clara Mae trail behind, exchanging remarks with the gang.

Ralph and friends are seated at a table. Immediately a beady-eyed waiter with Vaseline hair oil hands them the Red Rooster à la carte deluxe menu. He then stands back, smirking and waiting for the order.

WAITER
Could I get you gentlemen something to drink?

RALPH
(*uncertainly*)
Ah . . . uh . . . Make it a triple.

WAITER
(*raised eyebrows*)
A triple?

NARRATOR
A triple was a drink I'd always heard my father order. It was the only drink I knew.

RALPH
(*in answer to question from waiter*)
Yeah, on the rocks.

Camera pans to Wanda, who is ogling Ralph with great, swimming, lovesick eyes.

WAITER
(*to Schwartz*)
And you, sir?

SCHWARTZ
I'll have the same.

WAITER
And for the ladies . . . may I suggest the specialty of the house?
A Grenadine Jungle Flip?

Clara Mae smiles and bats her eyelashes.

CLARA MAE
Oh, I think I would like that very much.

WANDA
Ah . . . I'll have the same.

CU of Arlita at the piano, shot through the large aquarium atop the piano. Her platinum hair gleams. Tropical fish float back and forth through the tank.

Schwartz turns around in his chair, gives Arlita the eye. She returns his scrutiny with a small, enigmatic smile. Schwartz leans forward toward Ralph.

SCHWARTZ
Hey, Ralph. She's some tomato, huh?

RALPH
Yes. I'd like to get ahold of her!

Wanda and Clara Mae giggle, put their heads together.

WANDA
I'll bet that's not her real hair.

CLARA MAE
Yeah, but she's a good piano player.

The waiter returns with the drinks and places pink concoctions before the girls.

WANDA
Thank you.

WAITER
And for the gentlemen—triples.

Ralph picks up glass placed by waiter in front of him. Clara Mae giggles and Wanda smiles dreamily. Ralph brings the bourbon to his lips and downs it in a single devil-may-care draught, the way Gary Cooper used to do in the Silver Dollar Saloon.

NARRATOR

A screaming, ninety-proof rocket searing savagely down my gullet. For an instant I sat stunned, unable to comprehend what had happened.

CU Ralph's face. He is absolutely expressionless.

WAITER

(*voice echoing*)
Another drink, gentlemen?

CU bartender's hands as he pours drinks.

SFX: "The Call to the Post" played on a tinny trumpet.

Cut to table. Ralph downs second drink in the same manner as the first.

NARRATOR
For an instant it seemed as though this one wasn't going to be as lethal as the first. Then . . .

Cut to film clip of exploding lava.

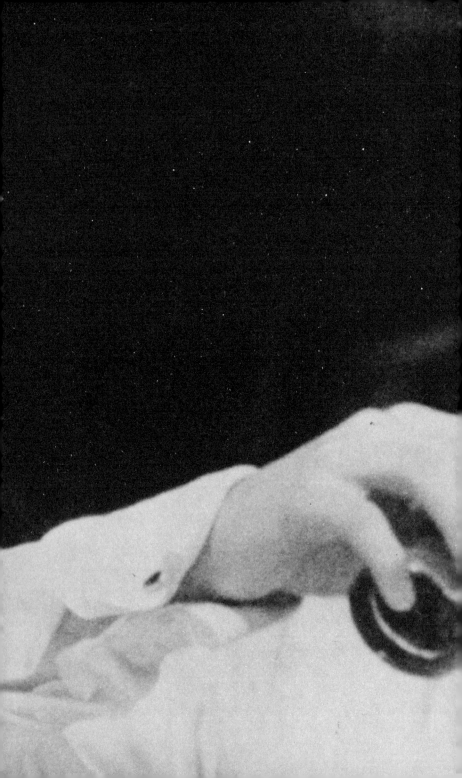

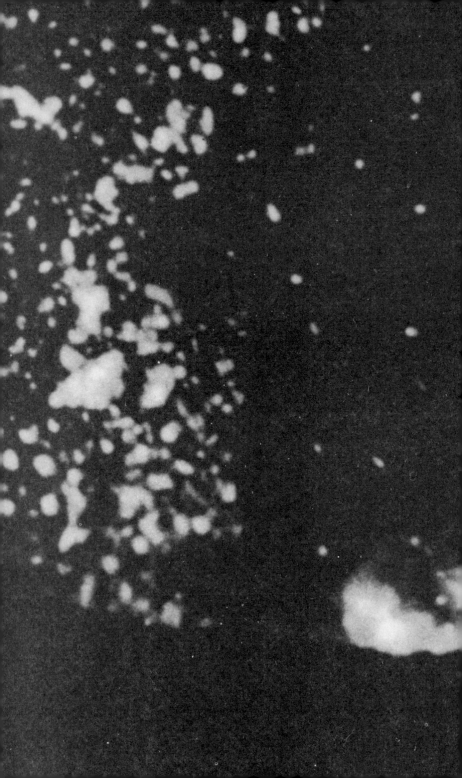

Cut back to Ralph's face. He is paralyzed.

Music becomes distorted.

Cut to Arlita, shot through distortion lens.

NARRATOR
My diaphragm heaved convulsively, jiggling my cummerbund.

Cut to lava, exploding even higher, throwing glowing flames skyward.

Cut to shot of Wanda and Clara Mae from Ralph's point of view, their faces appear to swim in and out of frame and in and out of focus.

Cut to exploding lava, flames shooting higher and higher.

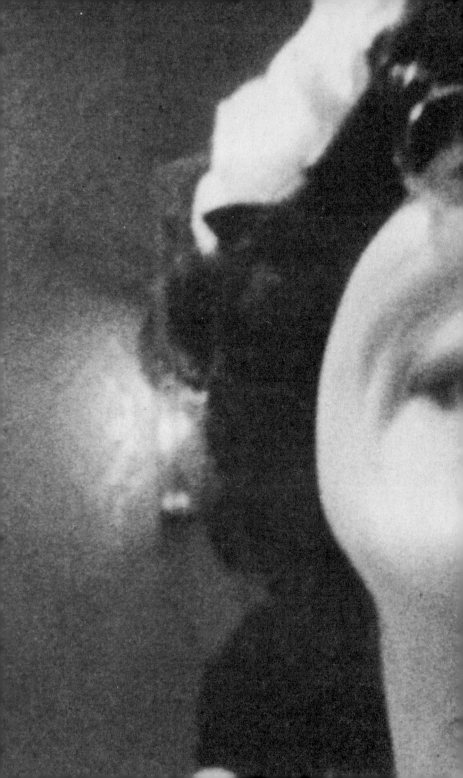

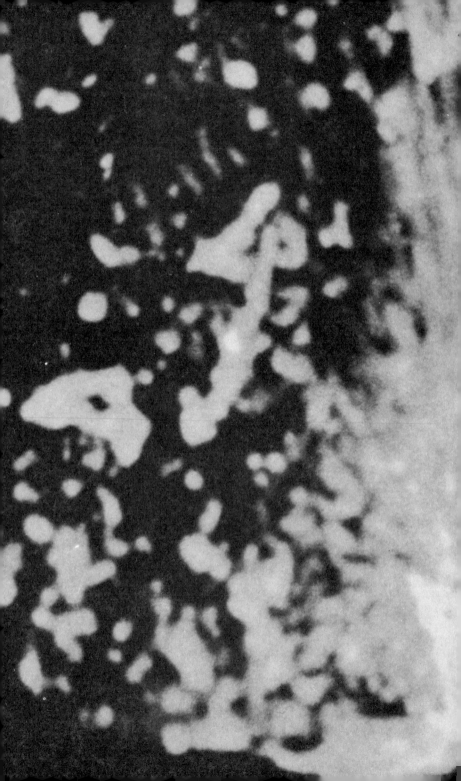

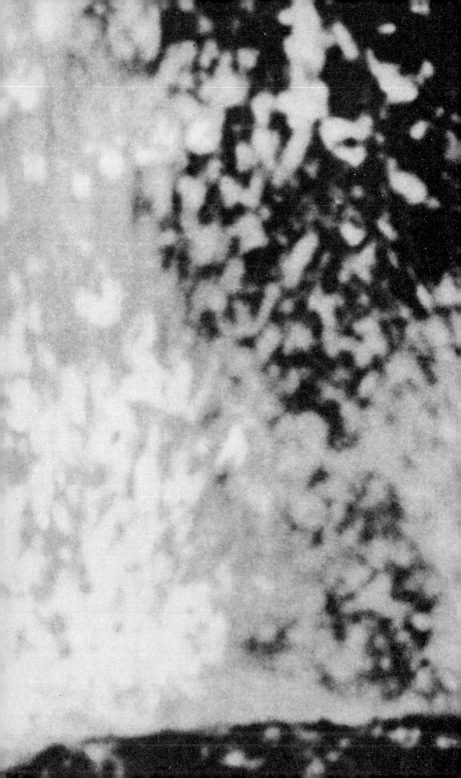

NARRATOR

The forest fire in my gut was out of control. Schwartz began to shrink; his face was purple-red.

CU Schwartz. He is trying with the terrible patience of a drunk, to shake salt out of the wrong end of the salt shaker.

CU Wanda. Her face is distorted, seeming all mouth and gleaming eyeglasses and teeth.

WANDA

(*voice sounds far away*)
Isn't this romantic? This is the most wonderful, wonderful night in all of our very own lives.

CU of table. The food has arrived. Many CU shots of food; lamb chops swimming in grease, lumpy mashed potatoes.

CU Wanda. She is eating spaghetti and the spaghetti trails in long strings off her fork.

SFX piano music, becoming more and more discordant. The room seems to lurch sideways. Swinging in and out of the picture, Ralph sees Flick drinking and eating a large cheeseburger. The room begins to swing dizzily around and around.

RALPH
(*his face blank, voice polite, controlled*)
Uh, I hope you ladies will excuse us. Mr. Schwartz and I will repair to the Men's Room.

WANDA AND CLARA
Yes, certainly.

Ralph and Schwartz rise slowly and carefully, their faces blank. They walk carefully away from the table.

Cut to men's-room door. Ralph and Schwartz approach slowly, then rush through door.

Cut to inside of men's room. Ralph and Schwartz try door of one of the two stalls. It is occupied. They turn and both pile desperately into the remaining stall. We see nothing but their feet. Another pair of feet rushes in. It is Flick. He joins them.

Sounds of retching, heaving, and gagging.

NARRATOR
Lamb chops, bourbon, turnips, mashed potatoes, cole slaw . . . all of it came rushing out of me in a great roaring torrent. Up came the cheeseburgers, the rum and Cokes, pretzels, potato chips, orange punch, a corned beef sandwich—that was last week!

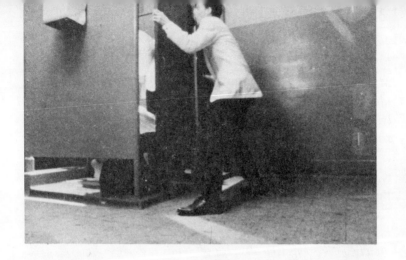

More retching and groaning. Someone comes in (we see only his feet), sees what is going on and leaves hastily. Ralph is now lying on the floor. Flick's legs, knees sagging, can be seen protruding from the stall.

NARRATOR
But then as suddenly as it had started, it was all over. I was seventy-four pounds lighter.

Slowly with great difficulty, Ralph hauls himself to his feet.

NARRATOR
It was the absolute high point of the Junior Prom. Everything else was anticlimax.

The door opens and, ashen-faced, the three slowly return to their tables. They look as though nothing has happened.

Cut to outside Wanda's house. Ralph and Wanda slowly come up the walk, go up on the porch. We hear a violin melody and the chirp of crickets.

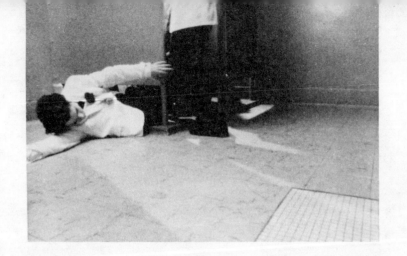

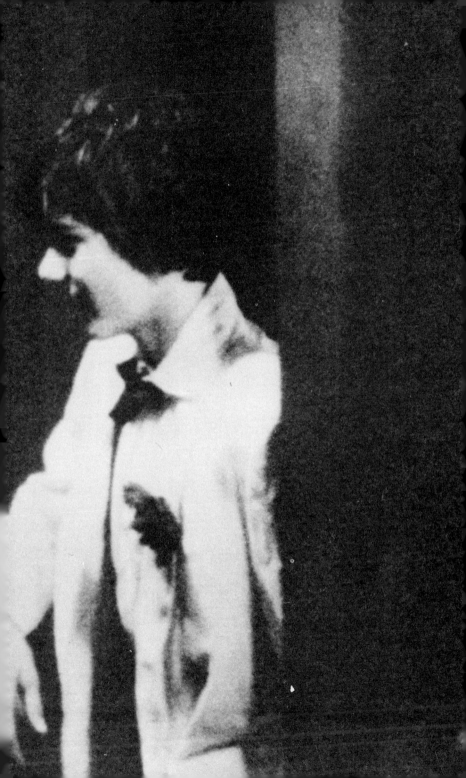

WANDA

It was the most wonderful, wonderful night of my life. I always dreamed the Prom would be like this.

RALPH

(*weakly*)
Me too.

Violins play softly.

Wanda's eyes close dreamily. Ralph, swaying slightly, leans forward.

NARRATOR

I knew what was expected of me.

Extreme CU of Wanda's face, eyes closed, lips pursed for a kiss.

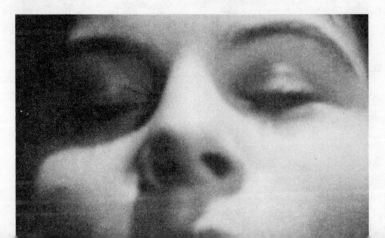

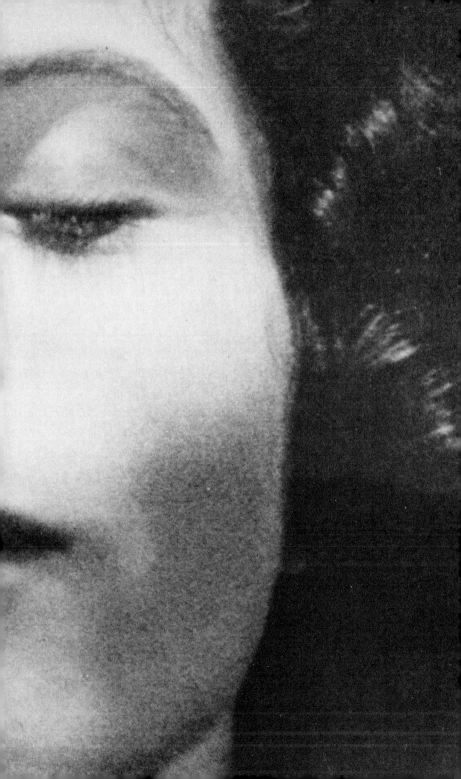

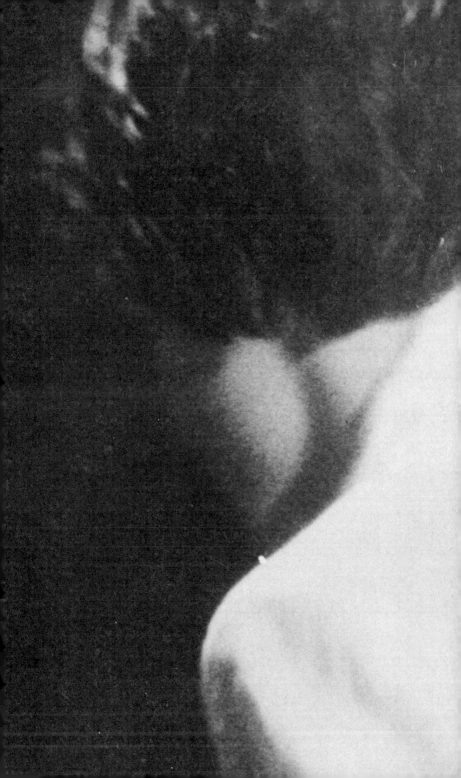

RALPH

(*blurts*)
'By!

Ralph gets off porch fast, backpedaling desperately.

WANDA
'By.

Ralph jumps into car and races off, leaving Wanda staring after him alone on the porch.

Camera cuts to street as Ralph's car screeches around corner and stops in front of vacant lot. Camera is on far side of car, but we see door open and Ralph fall out. Sound of retching can be heard.

Dissolve to kitchen where father is drinking coffee. It is 5 A.M. He is wearing his fishing hat and has fishing tackle leaning against the table. Sound of car pulling in is heard.

A few seconds later Ralph enters. In the cold light of day we see how disheveled he really looks. He stands in the doorway—a wreck—muddy pants, maroon-streaked vomit-stained white coat, open shirt, dirty hands, white-faced, and looking awful.

The Old Man looks up.

OLD MAN
You look like you had a helluva Prom.

RALPH
I sure did.

OLD MAN

(*needling him*)
You want somethin' to eat?

RALPH
I don't think so.

OLD MAN
Better get some sleep. You'll feel better in a coupla days, when
your head stops banging. (*He smiles*) I know.

*Ralph slowly walks through kitchen and heads up the stairs. His
cummerbund falls off and lies at the bottom of the stairs. We
hear Mickey Eisley playing "Good Night, Sweetheart." Ralph
lets coat fall to the floor at the base of the staircase, slowly begins
to climb stairs.*

NARRATOR

The male human animal, skulking through the impenetrable fetid jungle of Kidhood, learns early in the game just what sort of animal he is. The jungle he stalks is a howling, tangled wilderness, infested with crawling, flying, leaping, nameless dangers.

Through this all we continue to hear "Good Night, Sweetheart" and see Ralph climbing the stairs.

He daily does battle with horrors and emotions that he will spend the rest of his life trying to forget or suppress. Or recapture. His jungle is a wilderness he will never fully escape, but those first early years, when the bloom is on the peach and the milk teeth have just barely departed, are the crucial days in the Great Education of Life.

Camera holds on white coat as Ralph disappears up the stairs.

Mat in credits.

Cut to driver/narrator, the grown-up Ralph.

DRIVER

Oh, that great coat. You know, sometimes I wake up at three o'clock in the morning and I can still feel that coat pulling across the shoulders, and I'll bet it's still in action. I wonder whose party it's gonna be at tonight. (*He chuckles*) Oh, Daphne. Nothing ever quite works out. (*Chuckles again*)

Camera pans out car window, picks up billboard: "Air Force Jobs Are Super." It is a huge air-force recruiting ad.

CU of driver.

DRIVER

(*he laughs*)
The Army. The *Army!* Now that's a whole different ball game. Did I ever tell you about the time I was in this radar company, and they had us all lined up for a VD lecture. (*He chuckles.*) Well . . .

Camera pulls back to reveal car going down the road. It slowly becomes lost in traffic.

The Film Ends

AIR FORCE JOBS ARE SUPER

Call 800-447-4700 toll free

"The Phantom of the Open Hearth"

Written by
JEAN SHEPHERD

Produced and directed by
FRED BARZYK
DAVID LOXTON

Associate producer
OLIVIA TAPPAN

Director of photography
PETER HOVING

Associate director and editor
DICK BARTLETT

Art director
JOHN WRIGHT STEVENS

Costume designer
JENNIFER VON MAYRHAUSER

Lighting director
STEVEN SILVERMAN

Casting

JAY WOLF

Production manager

DARLENE MASTRO

Production associate

LEIGH BROWN

Production co-ordinator

DAN BEACH

Music consultant

JOHN Q. ADAMS

Audio

STEVE SHANE

Assistant cameraman

MARTY OSTROW

Gaffer

RAFFAELLO FERRUCCI

Lighting assistants

PAUL RAILA
MICHAEL DICK
DAVID WHITTIER

Hairdresser

JOSEPH M. GRIFONI

Makeup

ROBERT PHILIPPE

Assistant art director

R. J. FRANCO

Costume assistants

MARLA SCHWEPPE
BONNIE BAKER

Wardrobe

CANDACE CHASE

Props

ALAN CHAPMAN

Assistants to the producer

MIKE BLOECHER
JANET OLIVER

Production secretaries

MARY FENSTERMACHER
STEPHANIE WEIN

Audio mixer

RICHARD VORISEK

Assistant editor

ALEX MOSCU

Production assistance provided by

BOSTON AND MAINE RAILROAD
BRITISH LEYLAND MOTORS
CONCORD ACADEMY
INLAND STEEL
READ AND WHITE
THE TWELVE EIGHTY RESTAURANT

Executive producer for "Visions"

BARBARA SCHULTZ

Film-to-Photo conversion by

MARY FENSTERMACHER